ORIGINS OF THE
MODERN CHINESE STATE

ORIGINS OF THE
MODERN CHINESE STATE

PHILIP A. KUHN

STANFORD UNIVERSITY PRESS

Stanford, California

Origins of the Modern Chinese State was originally published in French in 1999 as *Les Origines de l'Etat chinois moderne* by Philip A. Kuhn, translated from the English and presented by Pierre-Etienne Will, Collection Cahiers des Annales c 1999 by Editions de l'Ecole de Hautes Etudes en Sciences Sociales (Paris). The present edition has been modified by the author in a number of matters of detail and presentation.

English edition ©2002 by the Board of Trustees of the Leland Stanford Junior University

Printed in the United States of America

isbn 0-8047-4283-9 (cloth : alk. paper)
isbn 0-8047-4929-9 (pbk. : alk. paper)

This book is printed on acid-free, archival-quality paper.

Original printing 2002

Last figure below indicates year of this printing:
11   10   09   08   07   06   05   04
      03

Typeset at Stanford University Press in 11/14 Galliard

In Memory of Benjamin I. Schwartz

Preface

The chapters of this book originated as lectures that I de-
livered at the Collège de France during January 1994. I am
most grateful for the generosity of my French hosts, especially Pierre-Étienne Will, Professor of Modern Chinese
History at the Collège, who made our time in Paris thor-
oughly delightful. He not only gave unstintingly of his
hospitality, but also contributed in countless ways to the
book itself. Besides translating and editing the lectures, he
made numerous improvements in the content. The resulting volume owes much to his efforts. His introduction to
the French edition,[1] "Entre Présent et Passé," though not
translated here, was a source of many insights to me and
greatly improved the present text.

   I am also indebted to my brother David, who kindly
prepared the French text for my lectures. Others who read

[1]Philip A. Kuhn, *Les Origines de l'État Chinois Moderne*. Traduit et présenté par
Pierre-Étienne Will (Paris: Cahiers des Annales, distributed by Armand Colin,
1999). Earlier versions of Chapters 1 and 2 appeared as "Ideas Behind China's Modern State" in *Harvard Journal of Asiatic Studies* 55.2 (1995), pp. 295–337.

all or parts of the manuscript and offered valuable comments were Peter K. Bol, Ch'en Yung-fa, Prasenjit Duara, Mark C. Elliott, Lin Man-houng, and William T. Rowe. Finally, I have benefited from the help and advice of Ch'en Hsi-yuan, Ju Deyuan, Kong Xiangji, and Wang Xiangyun. Muriel Bell of the Stanford University Press has been a marvellously supportive editor. None of those who contributed so much to this work is in any way responsible for its remaining shortcomings.

P.A.K.

Cambridge, Massachusetts,
January 2001

Contents

ORIGINS OF THE
MODERN CHINESE STATE

Introduction

What is Chinese about China's modern state? The revolutions and reforms that produced it were surely influenced by forces from abroad; indeed, the main point of making a modern state was to resist foreign domination by using some of the foreigners' own technologies of dominance, both material and societal. The enterprise seemed to require mobilizing the energies of the people, rewriting the rules of political competition, and intensifying state control over society and economy. These goals were considered necessary for China's survival—even more necessary than the integrity of her inherited culture. That history be sacrificed to power has seemed inescapable to Chinese of the modern age.

Yet the character of China's modern state has been shaped decisively by the flow of its internal history. Political activists of the nineteenth century were already dealing with questions of participation, competition, and control in the context of conditions inherited from the eighteenth century and earlier.

The essays that follow suggest that they were responding to a persistent *domestic* constitutional agenda that links the late imperial with the modern age. By "constitutional" I mean a set of concerns about the legitimate ordering of public life; and by "agenda," a will to grapple with these concerns in action. Though the constitutional agenda of the early nineteenth century was expressed in terms proper to that age, its underlying structure links it to the agendas of later generations.

Three issues that engaged men of the late Qing have endured and indeed seem to have gained urgency from modern conditions: How was broadened political participation to be reconciled with enhancing the power and legitimacy of the state? How could political competition be reconciled with the concept of a public interest? And how could the fiscal demands of the state be reconciled with the needs of local society? This modern constitutional agenda did not originate solely in the foreign crisis, but in the many-sided domestic crisis that beset the late empire.

The Crisis of the 1790s

The 1790s were not an abrupt turning point in Chinese history, but a culmination of trends that were leading the Qing empire—and perhaps the late imperial order—to disaster. Together, these trends constituted a long-term change in China's political economy: a change that led some members of the literati elite to understand that constitutional issues were at stake. These issues later came to be understood, in China and abroad, as aspects of the Western invasion (politely known as the "opening" of China) that began in the days of the Opium War and continued into the twentieth century. There are reasons to believe, however, that arguments for creating a modern nation to resist the West were part of a larger discussion emerging within China itself. What lay in the background of that discussion can be illustrated through the crisis of the 1790s, which evidently provoked some among the literati elite to think in constitutional terms.

In October 1795, the 84-year-old emperor Qianlong proclaimed that he would abdicate the throne after a sixty-year reign.[1] As his heir he named his fifteenth son, who was to rule under the reign title Jiaqing. Of Qing dynasty monarchs, only his grandfather, Kangxi, had reigned as long, and no monarch more gloriously. Qianlong proudly bequeathed Jiaqing a "prosperous age" in which the Chinese people had doubled in number, and Beijing's control had penetrated deep into Central Asia. Yet his son inherited not prosperity, but a cascade of troubles.

Qianlong had abdicated in name, but not in fact. How natural, in a Chinese setting, that the old man should have continued to rule behind the scenes as "Grand Emperor," acting upon the most vital documents and issuing commands unabated. In a land where filial piety was the virtue of virtues, what monarch could rule while his sire lived? So the old monarch's rule, as distinct from his reign, lasted until his death in 1799. The new emperor had to report all important matters to his father through the chief Grand Councillor, Heshen. An imperial favorite for two decades

[1] "Qianlong" was not actually the emperor's name, but the name of his reign-period, which lasted from 1736 to 1796.

past, Heshen had used his position to reward followers, to punish enemies, and to weave a patronage network that reached into imperial treasuries throughout the realm. As the Grand Emperor's strength waned, Heshen controlled the court through a *de facto* regency. The new emperor was subject not only to his father, but to his father's chief courtier.

For weak leadership at the center it was the worst of times. In 1795, the unstable frontier society in the rugged borderlands of the west erupted in popular rebellions that were to harass imperial forces for most of a decade. Floods of the Yellow and Yangzi rivers had swept over central and eastern provinces beginning in 1789. Meanwhile, an equally portentous disaster had its small beginnings at the subtropical port of Guangzhou, where trade with Britain was outgrowing its administrative restraints. There, British traders were learning to pay for tea exports by shipping opium from India. This was a trade with a future. When the Grand Emperor died in February 1799, he left an empire in distress.

The crisis of the 1790s arose from the very triumphs of Qianlong's reign: the flourishing trade and the burgeoning population of the "prosperous age." The abundance of silver in the economy, drawn in by foreign trade at varying rates over two centuries, but especially after the 1780s, fueled a slow, steady inflation of prices. Local government became more costly, but the system for paying those costs remained inadequate. A brave attempt by Qianlong's father in the 1720s to create a reliable tax base for official salaries had failed: reliance on informal surtaxes was too deeply ingrained, the rising expenses of government too pressing.

These rising expenses were due partly to the increasing

luxury of official lives, especially at the apex of the system, where Qianlong and his courtiers set the extravagant tone. Through Heshen's patronage network, the wherewithal at each level was siphoned from the level below: "gifts" to superiors fit neatly into the customary patron-client networks of official life. Courtiers took from governors, who in turn took from prefects, who took from county magistrates. Ultimately, those who paid were the common people.[2]

Throughout his long career, Qianlong had been wary of court factions led by imperial favorites. Yet the Grand Emperor of the late 1790s was no longer the alert and resolute monarch of earlier decades; Heshen, as chief Grand Councillor, was free to manipulate imperial policy and resources. With his master's connivance, he devised a system of "fines" for extorting money from provincial officials, the proceeds of which he shared with Qianlong.[3] In effect, the aging monarch and his favorite were running a second taxation system for their joint enrichment. During the 1790s, Qianlong's unwavering patronage of Heshen overrode his hostility to factions. Heshen's might indeed be called a "hyperfaction," because it had impregnable protection from the ultimate powerholder. Thus fortified, it spread far and wide in the risk-averse bureaucracy that the throne's own policies had fostered, and the few who dared challenge it did so to their grief. Only after the death of Qianlong himself, in 1799, could Heshen and his faction be overthrown.

Down in the counties, from which the wealth was ultimately siphoned, corruption of local government was ram-

---

[2]Feng Zuozhe, *Heshen pingzhuan* (Beijing: Zhongguo qingnian chubanshe, 1998), pp. 152–67, 229–30.

[3]Lin Xinqi, "Qianlong xunzheng yu Heshen shanquan," *Qingshi yanjiu tongxun*, 1986, no. 2, pp. 17–19.

rampant
corruption

pant. "The misdeeds of county magistrates are a hundred times worse than ten or twenty years ago," wrote the outspoken official Hong Liangji in 1798—obliquely invoking the period of Heshen's ascendancy.[4] Hong went on to accuse magistrates of inciting farmers to rebellion by accusing them of sectarianism and then extorting money from them.

over population
farming
migration

The long arm of Heshen's second taxation system pressed heavily upon a society already feeling the effects of overcrowding and land shortage. A population increase from about 143 million in 1741 to over 300 million in 1794 (an average annual increase of about 3.2 million)[5] was the prime mover of the 1790s crisis. But what made such an immense expansion possible? Although it undoubtedly owed much to the long period of internal peace since the consolidation of Manchu rule in the 1680s, new ways to make a living also helped an expanding population feed itself. The arrival of Europeans in East and Southeast Asia since the early sixteenth century had created a network of foreign trade that nourished China's internal markets with silver from Japan and the New World. The nationwide spread of markets enabled China's farmers to supplement their incomes by producing handicrafts (mainly textiles) in their homes and by growing cash crops for sale. New crops from the Americas (maize, sweet potatoes, tobacco) helped them bring fresh land under cultivation, particularly unirrigable uplands and hillsides. The eighteenth century accordingly became China's greatest age of internal migra-

[4]Hong Liangji, "Zheng xiejiao shu," in He Changling, ed., *Huangchao jingshi wenbian* (Shanghai: Hongwen ge, 1898), 88.7–7b.
[5]Guo Songyi, "Qingdai de renkou zengzhang he renkou liuqian," *Qingshi luncong*, No. 5 (1984), pp. 103–38.

tion, as land-poor farmers moved not only into the hilly uplands, but also into less populated areas along the interprovincial frontiers. Yet despite massive migration and land clearance, the land-population ratio had sunk precariously low by the last decades of the Qianlong reign.[6]

Overcrowding brought ecological troubles: expanding agriculture deforested the watersheds of the great river systems, so that tons of silt eroded into the rivers and raised their diked beds ever higher above the surrounding countryside. Beginning with a vast flood in 1778, the Yellow River overwhelmed human efforts to contain it. Serious floods continued through the 1780s and 1790s. Twelve occurred between 1780 and 1799; and from 1796 to 1799, they were annual events. Because they coincided with Heshen's rise to power, men at the time believed that corrupt river-management officials were lining their pockets with funds meant for diking and dredging.[7]

Migration of land-poor farmers into the border regions of western China had produced another scourge of the times: interethnic conflict. Pressure by immigrant farmers and merchants sparked uprisings among minority peoples such as the Miao, who revolted in 1795 against Han officials and usurers. A year later, the recently settled society of the rugged border between Hubei, Sichuan, and Shaanxi was set ablaze by the greed and cruelty of local officials. Led by devout folk-Buddhist sectarians, the White Lotus rebellion broke out in 1796 and stood off Qing armies for eight years.

[6]*Ibid.*, p. 104.
[7]Shuilibu Huanghe shuili weiyuanhui, comp., *Huanghe shuili shi shuyao* (Beijing: Shuili chubanshe, 1982), pp. 310–20. Sun Wenliang et al., *Qianlong di* (Changchun: Jilin wenshi chupanshe, 1993), p. 508.

In both cases, misgovernment by money-hungry officials and their staffs compounded the miseries of crowding and land shortage; and above it all was the relentless financial pressure exerted by the Heshen network at Beijing.

Three Constitutional Dilemmas of the Late Empire

The crisis of the 1790s could easily be pictured as the nemesis of dynastic glory and extravagance, a retribution for corrupt official behavior and extravagant living. These vices, along with the senility of the sovereign and the greed of his minister, must have satisfied those who speculated about causes: conventional answers with ample precedents in history. Yet some seemed to have sensed a deeper menace: the decline of a polity that was increasingly unequal to its tasks. Perhaps it took the many-sided crisis of the 1790s to make men aware of what lay beneath particular events. What once had seemed accidental (a corrupt official, an ill-maintained dike, a senile emperor) was seen to be systemic; what had seemed local (a misgoverned county, an inter-ethnic clash) was perceived as national in scope.

Underlying the constitutional agenda of modern times were three critical dilemmas, all products of social and political developments of the Qing period: (1) how to animate a politically intimidated governing elite to confront abuses of power that harmed both government and society; (2) how to harness or control the political energies of the mass of educated men who could not be absorbed by careers in government; (3) how to govern a huge, complex society with a small field administration. It is worth considering whether these dilemmas of the late imperial system were so

✗ uncertainty avoidance

grave that fundamental changes were in store even had foreign aggression not occurred when it did.[8]

Confronting the abuse of power. The Chinese literati, chastened by living under a conquest regime, were schooled to *caution* caution. They received their cultural training from the Confucian classics, but their political training from the actual practice of Qing rule. There is no doubt that alien rule—particularly under the touchy Qianlong—had made the Han literati circumspect and fearful.

Qianlong, alive to the real danger that his Manchu compatriots were becoming assimilated to Chinese ways and losing their special *élan* as a warrior elite, strove to *Manchuness* buck up Manchu consciousness ("Manchuness") by exhortation and by literary projects for cultural self-awareness.[9] The other side of his truculence was a hypersensitivity to ethnic slurs from the subject literati, who soon learned that words, especially their allusive edges, could be fatal. The faintest hint of disrespect toward Manchu dominion could bring a writer's neck under the axe, and Qianlong made examples of those who had allegedly impugned the legitimacy of the dynasty by obscure written allusions. Such "literary cases," extending back to the 1750s, culminated in the 1770s

---

[8]Anyone who doubts that big changes were in store need look no further than the doctrines and policies of the Taiping Rebellion (1851–64). These included (1) a more thoroughing penetration of local government into society through a finely meshed system of local headmen; and (2) a redefinition of the monarchy's relationship to the elite by tying the elite into a system of theocratic control that was potentially far more draconian than the monarch-literati relationship under the Confucian empire. Of these, the first was drawn from ancient Chinese sources; and the second, from the messianic Christianity acquired by the Taiping leadership from Western missionaries. The Taiping theocracy was inspired by Western evangelism, but there was nothing "Western" about the way it was applied.

[9]Pamela Kyle Crossley, *Orphan Warriors: Three Manchu Generations and the End of the Qing World* (Princeton, N.J.: Princeton University Press, 1990), p. 21.

in a nationwide literary inquisition. Even the most far-fetched interpretation of a literary passage could not be disputed if it came from the throne. The lesson was not lost upon the literati. A Korean visitor discovered in 1780 that those he met were painfully circumspect. "Even about the most commonplace affairs, they burn the records of their conversations without leaving a scrap of paper. The Chinese are not alone in this; the Manchus are even worse."[10]

At a more basic level, however, caution was bred into the political values of the literati themselves. If resistance to power abuse requires constitutional sanction for getting together in political groups, then it is not surprising that the elite was unable to cope with Heshen. If fears of giving ethnic offense were not enough to keep critics quiet, there was the fear of being stigmatized as a "faction." Ironically the "faction" brush could be used to tar any combination that opposed the faction currently patronized by the throne. What was it about the charge of "faction" that made it so effective a weapon in the hands of the ruler? Part of its power came from the elite's own acceptance of it. Most were loath to appear factional because it was received wisdom that factionalism at court had undermined the preceding Ming regime in the early seventeenth century and had led indirectly to the Manchu conquest. And "faction" per se had a disreputable ring. The Confucian tag that superior men "were sociable but abjured factions"[11] was an ex-

[marginal note: resistance to power abuse]

---

[10]Min Tu-ki, *National Polity and Local Power: The Transformation of Late Imperial China* (Cambridge, Mass: Harvard University Press, 1989), p. 5. Min's chapter on "The *Jehol Diary* and the Character of Ch'ing Rule" (pp. 1–19) recounts the discoveries of Pak Chi-won about the inner thoughts of Chinese literati on politics and scholarship.

[11]The phrase is from *Confucian Analects*, XV.21, in James Legge, trans., *The Four Books: Confucian Analects, The Great Learning, The Doctrine of the Mean, and the*

cellent way for any executive to discourage his subordinates from forming cliques; but it was belied by the real situation on all levels of government.

Factions in the eighteenth-century bureaucracy were generally based not on shared opinions about policy, but on ties of kinship, regional origin, and academic patronage.[12] To the monarchy, the last of these was the most vexing: the civil-service examination system was a veritable faction factory. Not only did the examiner-examinee relationship create patron-client networks; the power of highly placed patrons to manipulate or "fix" examination results could also serve as a catalyst for factionalism. Beyond officialdom, factions flourished spontaneously in the soil of Chinese life. Kinship, region, and master-disciple groupings served as seedbeds for factions, which became obnoxious to rulers once they became powerful enough to limit royal authority or resources. It was impossible, however, to stamp them out. To stigmatize them as selfishly inclined toward "private" interest was only a partial solution; but, from the powerholder's point of view, it was better than nothing—and by the 1790s had effectively narrowed the options of any who might be inclined to oppose the abuse of power at the top. A whiff of sedition was enough to discourage concerted political action. Factions existed, but to display them overtly in politics was risky.

Manchu monarchs took a hard line against factions, particularly Qianlong's father, Yongzheng—who, having risen

Works of Mencius (Shanghai: The Chinese Book Co., 1933, reprint, New York: Paragon Book Reprint Corp., 1966).

[12]Sun Wenliang et al., *Qianlong ti*, pp. 131–41; Gao Xiang, *Kang-Yong-Qian sandi tongzhi sixiang yanjiu* (Beijing: Zhongguo renmin daxue chubanshe, 1995), pp. 386ff.

Factions to royalty

to power through a venomous factional struggle in the early eighteenth century, understood the dangers of factions to royal authority. Men formed factions out of envy and personal ambition, he pronounced, and then could not "accept the ruler's preferences." How can officials be considered loyal and public-spirited when they "deny their sovereign and work for their own interests?"[13] At the core of this self-protective rationale lay the principle that there was only one correct view of the public interest: the one identified by the only man with dispassionate sympathies and elevated perspectives. Such a view could hardly emerge from contention among disparate opinions, still less from competition among private (read "selfish") interests. Qianlong, too, developed a lifelong dislike of factions; early in his reign, he had to cope with the personal followings of two old advisers inherited from his father. Though he may have imagined that he had done away with the old factions and scared off new ones, factionalism came back to plague him grievously (the Heshen case) in his last years, when his vigor was waning.

To be sure, high officials were able to offer their recommendations to the monarch on all sorts of administrative policies, and in fact were required to do so. Qing rulers were far from being isolated despots, bereft of official advice.[14] Yet

[13]"On Factions" (1724), quoted in David S. Nivison, "Ho-shen and His Accusers," in David Nivison and Arthur Wright, eds., *Confucianism in Action* (Stanford, Calif.: Stanford University Press, 1959), pp. 225–26. Nivison is quoting *Da Qing Shizong Xian Huangdi shengxun*, 19.10a.

[14]Helen Dunstan, "'The Autocratic Heritage' and China's Political Future: A View from a Qing Specialist" *East Asian History* No.12 (1996) pp. 79–104. Pierre-Étienne Will, "Entre présent et passé," in Kuhn, *Les Origines de l'État Chinois Moderne*, pp. 54–55.

the Qing communications system worked through dyadic
links between a monarch and each of his ministers. Authorized channels of communication with the throne were narrow and tightly regulated. In the eighteenth century, any
concerted, sustained combination in support of a policy line
or an appointment would have been highly suspect.

Did the literati themselves doubt that the public interest
was unitary and exclusive? The famous example of literati
resistance to despotism at court (the "Donglin" movement
of the 1620s) suggests that they did not. That episode involved a faction of literati and officials who were determined to gain control over the court in Beijing by ma-
nipulating appointments and inserting its partisans into office through the examination system. The rallying cry was
to challenge the "evil" tyranny of a court eunuch. If one fo-
cuses only on the Donglin clique's staunch resistance to
what they considered tyranny, one easily overlooks that its
own premises were a mirror-image of what it opposed.
When they themselves held office, Donglin partisans ruthlessly purged the bureaucracy of their opponents; neither
power-sharing nor a plurality of interests was considered
acceptable. Only one public interest existed (defined in a
righteous rhetoric of personal ethics), and martyrdom was
an acceptable way to defend it. The movement and its fate
illustrate the winner-take-all outlook of factional warfare; it
was factionalism without a framework that could have
moderated and conciliated differences. In Qing times, the
Donglin legacy had become a cautionary tale about how
factional conflict damaged the public interest and state stability. For the sake of the literati's social position—which
was buttressed by a wide array of late imperial institutions

and policies—that stability was as precious to them as to the throne.[15]

The Heshen episode itself was enormously destabilizing to the regime, in terms of both elite morale and public legitimacy. How then could such abuse of power be resisted? To combine against it in a nonfactional way seemed a contradiction in terms. Nevertheless, after Heshen's fall in 1799, literati began to come up with promising responses. One was to broaden the political horizon of the literati by promoting practical techniques of governance in a manner free of moralistic pretensions. Such an approach would encourage participation while remaining implicitly loyalist and without taint of faction. Collaboration of like-minded literati could also be masked by genteel cultural formats, such as poetry circles or shrine-worshiping associations, some of which harbored partisan agendas. Finally, there was the farfetched option of looking to participation by broader reaches of the cultural elite. Such a resort, adopted eagerly at the end of the nineteenth century, was but dimly glimpsed by the post-Heshen generation.

The political energies of the cultural elite. Overshadowing late-imperial society as a whole was the gross disparity between its large cultural elite and its small official elite. By cultural elite I mean those whom Benjamin Elman calls "classically literate": trained to read, explicate, and indeed memorize the canonical texts used in the civil-service ex-

[15]For a discussion of Ming factionalism and its effects on Qing literati, see Will, "Entre Présent et Passé," pp. 55–58. For a skeptical view of the Donglin movement, see Fritz Mote and Denis Twitchett, ed., *The Ming Dynasty, 1368–1644, Part I. The Cambridge History of China*, Vol. 7 (Cambridge: Cambridge University Press, 1988), pp. 532–45.

amination system; and to write essays and poetry in classical style—whether or not they ever passed an examination. By "official elite" I mean that tiny fraction of the cultural elite who had passed the top examination and been appointed to official posts.

Years spent mastering the demanding examination curriculum set the classically literate apart from most of their countrymen. Their numbers included, of course, all those who passed a civil-service examination at any level; but they also included the much larger number who tried and failed. Given the overwhelming disparity between candidates and quotas, it is not clear that passing or failing always indicated a significant gap in ability. One of the most striking points in Elman's study is that, from a social-cultural point of view, *how many passed* the examinations is not the most meaningful question to ask.[16] While the spread of wealth and education generated increasing numbers of classically literate men, the gateway quotas for examination degrees remained quite stable. Thus there arose a high level of career blockage and frustration among large numbers of men whose chance of ever entering officialdom was near the vanishing point. The following results are striking: at the licentiate level *and* at the provincial level (men who held *shengyuan* and *juren* degrees), there was a virtual standstill in career prospects. And the vast majority of the classically literate below the licentiate level were doomed to remain forever uncertified. So most classically literate men on all

---

[16]Elman estimates the total number of "classically literate" by the mid-nineteenth century as perhaps three million men, or less than one percent of the entire population. *A Cultural History of Civil Examinations in Late Imperial China* (Berkeley: University of California Press, 2000), p. 237.

levels had such minuscule chances of attaining official-elite status that they were permanently outside the state system, however able and ambitious they might be.[17]

There is no question but that the civil-service degrees of most literati were valuable to them mainly as official certifications of privileged social status. Even on the licentiate level, the privileges were considerable: lowered tax liability, immunity from corporal punishment, and a day-to-day ability to fend off bullying agents of local government. To help one's sons achieve degrees was also the most available way to ensure that one's family status was sustained or improved. No other investment was as valuable. In a society virtually without castes or inherited status, a civil-service degree was in fact the only way to certify membership in the elite on any scale of society.

That said, it is also evident that some literati turned their degree status toward activities that can be termed broadly political, outside the format of state service. In local communities, the licentiates were commonly involved in proxy tax-remittance and litigation, both of which were illegal and, in some instances, disruptive to local order from the government's point of view. But there were many legal options, too. Local literati without government jobs were the pool for a "parapolitical" elite (to use G.W. Skinner's term) that was active on the local level in a realm of officially sanc-

[17]Three categories of the educated but blocked can be discerned. At the lowest level, those seeking the lowest degree had a success rate of about 1.5 percent during the Qing period. Of licentiates sitting for the provincial (*juren*) examination, about 5 percent would pass. And of provincial graduates, about 0.8 percent succeeded in passing the metropolitan (*jinshi*) examination, the gateway to official elite status (that is, perhaps .008 percent of the whole cultural elite). In the Qing period (1644–1911) the chance of a man's passing all levels of examination was .01 percent of all candidates. Ibid., pp. 141–43, 662.

tioned power outside the official system.[18] Localism in many forms was indeed the natural arena for those shut out of national politics. Managing community projects, compiling local gazetteers, promoting and conserving local culture and history, were options increasingly attractive and available to members of the cultural elite in late-imperial times.

Beyond these local activities, however, we cannot avoid considering that a cultural elite of more than three million men had been schooled in a classical curriculum that had taught them that *educated men had a political vocation*. The examinations frequently reinforced this point by referring to national affairs (though generally not to contemporary affairs) and by including "policy" questions along with literary ones (not usually questions about current policy issues, but—perhaps even more important—questions relating to historical experiences of the imperial state).[19] Behind the constitutional agenda of the late empire, then, was a sizable stratum of educated men with at least a latent awareness of national affairs, but with no hope of participating in them. What channels of participation might be opened to them by the crisis of the age?

When Walter Bagehot described the nineteenth-century English as "an intelligent and political people" he meant that they had a sustained interest in public affairs, even though only a minority were franchised to participate in them.[20] Could this be said of the Chinese classically literate?

[18]For "parapolitical" see G. William Skinner, "Cities and the Hierarchy of Local Systems" in Skinner, ed., *The City in Late Imperial China* (Stanford, Calif.: Stanford University Press, 1977), pp. 336–44.

[19]Elman, *A Cultural History*, p. 9.

[20]Walter Bagehot, *The English Constitution* (London: Oxford University Press, 1949 [1872]), p. 65.

Certainly there were elements in their training and social position that tended to make them, in Bagehot's sense, "political." In this respect, there was more to unite than to divide them. Whether of high status or low, the literati shared a classical schooling in which the essentials of civic order and of good government permeated their texts. Therefore we should not be surprised to find some sense, among those out of office, that the difference between themselves and the official elite owed less to quality than to circumstance.

Was there any group that could respond to national challenges as a national constituency, a sort of proto-citizenry whose sense of a stake in the fate of their nation could mobilize them to greater participation? Although it was not until the fourth decade of the nineteenth century, in the context of resistance to the West, that the stirrings of such a constituency were visible, there are reasons to think that the potential for it lay not far beneath the surface. One group of literati, in particular, constituted a *de facto* non-official national elite: the provincial graduates, numbering about 10,000, of whom about 8,000 showed up *in the national capital* every three years to sit for the metropolitan examination.[21] Holders of provincial degrees were sensitized to national events by their pilgrimages, from every province, to Beijing, where they formed social and literary connections with their counterparts from other provinces, came into contact with serving officials, and immersed themselves in the capital rumor mill. In this sense, holders

---

[21]Elman, *A Cultural History* (p. 152), points out that the *juren* became essentially "down-classed" during Qing times, because in practical terms they were no longer appointable to low-level official posts; they had become a permanent candidate stratum.

of provincial degrees were not strictly "provincial" or "local" elites, but a national elite, aware of national issues and in contact with a cohort of others who were aware of them too. They were the group that were viewed by Wei Yuan (see Chapter 1) as established literati, sensitized to national events and conscious of their qualification to take part in them.[22]

The disparity between the large number of degree-holders and the small number of government posts to which they might be appointed had been inherited from the preceding Ming dynasty. Yet conditions of the eighteenth and nineteenth centuries made that disparity politically significant. The many-sided crisis of the 1790s and its aftermath encouraged the out-of-office national elite in statecraft studies. The mounting foreign crisis of the early nineteenth century offered that elite new opportunities for attacking the loyalty and integrity of powerholders. Perhaps most significant, the needs of reformist officials offered new opportunities for actual participation by *juren* in government through staff positions.

Although provincial graduates were not normally eligible for official appointment in Qing times, one notable

[22]There is also a case for including the lower-status but much larger group of "imperial academy students" (who held the purchased degree of *jiansheng*, and who numbered about 310,000 before 1850 and perhaps 430,000 after the Taiping Rebellion), who were eligible to compete in the provincial-level examination held in Beijing. Numbers of *jiansheng* who showed up in Beijing, from all over the country, for the Shuntian provincial examination varied from 2,000 to 7,000 in early Qing, then grew steadily: ten thousand examination cubicles were constructed in 1735, and in the late nineteenth century there were 14,000. See Susan Naquin, *Peking: Temples, Public Space, and Urban Identities, 1400–1900* (Berkeley: University of California Press, 2000), pp. 363, 416. For total numbers of *juren* and *jiansheng*, see Chang Chung-li, *The Chinese Gentry: Studies on Their Role in Nineteenth-Century Chinese Society* (Seattle: University of Washington Press, 1955), pp. 126, 137.

substitute route offered involvement in the actual practice of national affairs: the career of private secretary (*muyou*) to high officials. The *juren* were able to enter the inner circles of provincial-level administrators as social equals, to serve as a brain-trust for important projects. Note that two of the most prominent institutional reformers of the early nineteenth century, Wei Yuan and Bao Shichen (1775–1855) gained their reputations as advisers to high provincial officials while holding the *juren* degree. These men contributed policy initiatives, moreover, in respect to institutions of national scope—namely the salt monopoly and the Grain Transport Administration. In the course of the tumultuous nineteenth century, opportunities for *juren* like them increased greatly as the private staffs of high officials absorbed more free-floating administrative talent to cope with military and foreign-affairs crises. By the end of the century, the entourage of a governor-general might contain dozens of talented men with high political ambition but no orthodox entryway into the official elite.

I emphasize the "national" dimension of this *de facto* elite for two reasons. First, the crisis of the 1790s exposed historical crises of national scope. The extractive power of the Heshen machine diminished not only the efficiency of the bureaucracy nationwide, but also the stability of local communities in the farthest reaches of the empire. The popular rebellions of that era were touched off by the unappeasable financial appetites of local officials, which in turn were powerfully affected by the demands of the Heshen network anchored in the national capital. Even without Heshen, the fiscal mess in local government was a nationwide problem, whose extent had long been understood at the highest levels, as we shall see in Chapter 3. By the 1820s, malfunctions in nationally and regionally organized systems such as the salt monopoly and the Grain Transport Administration had seized the attention of literati and piqued their interest in national level solutions. Second, the economic disruptions caused by the foreign presence at Guangzhou and the eventual crisis of the Opium War spurred activism among cultural elites on all levels, whether in office or out. Some of the literati who were most concerned with the national dimensions of the domestic crisis in the immediate post-Heshen years became deeply involved in the foreign-affairs dimension of the national crisis as it intensified over the course of the nineteenth century.

Governing a huge society with a small bureaucracy. By the eighteenth century, it was evident that there existed a serious disparity between the ambitions and the capacities of the state: society had outgrown the political system that sought to govern it. This was no mere abstraction to Chinese of the late empire, but one that touched their livelihoods and their families' survival. In its extreme forms, it threatened the stability of local society and hence the security of the state.

The Manchu Qing regime had brought the authority of the throne, the discipline of the bureaucracy, and the efficiency of imperial communication to a level previously unknown in Chinese history. The inbuilt irony of this powerful, rationalized administrative system was that it was much more effective at the top than at the bottom.[23] For all

---

[23]For the "top" see Beatrice S. Bartlett, *Monarchs and Ministers: The Grand Council in Mid–Ch'ing China, 1723–1820* (Berkeley: University of California Press, 1991).

its administrative sophistication, it was only tenuously in control of subcounty government, and hence of its own fiscal base in local society.

The Qianlong demographic expansion placed unprecedented demands on an inexpansible local bureaucracy. Though the population had more than doubled, the number of county-scale units had barely changed at all. The result was that the size and complexity of county societies was drastically out of scale with the administrative forces charged with controlling and taxing them.[24] By the mid-eighteenth century, China's expanding, dynamic society and economy could barely be contained by its static political framework. Not only was the number of counties static; county bureaucratic staffs did not grow to meet the expanding needs of government. As the lowest bureaucratically certified imperial official, the county magistrate was dependent on a staff of local men who were neither evaluated nor disciplined by the central government.

Rising population and a relatively free market in land had made tax collection increasingly difficult and expensive. In fact it had raised the costs of all aspects of local administration, costs that had to be met by whatever the magistrate's agents could extract from the people. Tax collection was in the hands of low-status men who had to live, as it were, off the country. These were the hundreds of clerks and runners (including tax-collectors and process-servers) commonly employed by a county administration.

---

[24]G. William Skinner notes that the number of counties has remained amazingly constant since the eleventh century, even though (especially in recent centuries) the population has expanded both spatially and numerically. This he links to "a secular decline in governmental effectiveness from mid-T'ang times [ninth century] to the end of the imperial era. . . ." "Urban Development in Imperial China" in Skinner, ed., *The City in Late Imperial China*, p. 19.

This hard-working but generally despised group of functionaries was supported by fees and surtaxes levied by themselves directly on taxpayers—a system that invited abuse.

There were many reasons for the state *not* to expand its bureaucracy in step with population growth. There was the old faith in frugal government, a cherished marker of a heaven-favored dynastic regime. Then, deeply rooted in bureaucratic traditionalism, there was the tenacity of existing county-scale units (*zhou* and *xian*), a tenacity that perhaps had something to do with the established ritual cult affiliated with every county seat. Finally, there was the double identity of officials, who were both state administrators and cultural elite. To expand the regular bureaucracy in scale with the expanding workload of local government would have diluted the exclusivity of literati status. Officialdom was a "club" that defined itself not by its administrative functions alone, but also by its cultural distance from the uncouth and the unlettered. Members of this club made a particular point of scorning the petty functionaries who actually attended to the details of governing village China. Nothing in the self-image of the literati-bureaucrats would have been consistent with a broad expansion of the civil service corps.[25]

Taking into account the clerk-runner stratum, we can see that a denser local administration *did* emerge in late

[25]A high-level debate in 1729 over sub-county functionaries had simply finessed the question of expanding the official "club." At issue was a proposal to recruit "local officials" (*xiangguan*) from among the indigenous elite, to serve as links between the county magistrate and the people. Such functionaries, it seems to me, could hardly have been regarded as additions to the regular civil service corps. On this debate, see William T. Rowe, *Chen Hongmou: Elite Consciousness in Eighteenth-Century China* (Stanford, Calif.: Stanford University Press, 2001), pp. 345–46.

imperial times; but only by raising the transaction costs (including the social costs) of the revenue-collection and judicial systems to unacceptable heights.[26] Despite Beijing's repeated efforts to prohibit unauthorized fees or to claw them back, such fees were what sustained the daily operation of county government. The problem was probably insoluble within the prevailing ethos of "frugal government" and bureaucratic exclusivity. Nothing short of new institutions for state penetration into village society, or alternatively some form of local self-government that could oversee tax-collection in the community interest, could regulate this all-important nexus of state and society. The popular uprisings of the 1790s, partly occasioned by rampant taxation abuses, had already alerted Hong Liangji to the systemic problems of local governance. By the 1830s, the problem had worsened: tax rebellions were sparked by a currency imbalance precipitated by silver shortages in rural society, which in turn had been caused in part by the opium trade. What had been a chronic evil became an escalating disaster.

⌒

The chapters that follow suggest some of history's contributions to the distinctiveness of the modern Chinese state. This distinctiveness will not be presented as an inescapable "Chineseness," of which innate cultural qualities ensure that "China will always be China." That circular route can lead us to nothing interesting about history. Instead, each generation dealt with inherited constitutional problems in ways appropriate to its time. New constitutional problems

[26]On clerks and runners, see Bradly W. Reed, *Talons and Teeth: County Clerks and Runners in the Qing Dynasty* (Stanford, Calif.: Stanford University Press, 2000).

arose along the way, but they too outlasted the generation that first confronted them.

Chapter 1 questions the connection between broader political participation and state power. It explores the writings of the literatus Wei Yuan, who reinterpreted some of the most revered classical texts to construct a case for broadening the state's political base and, at the same time, for rousing his contemporaries from their political apathy. In the process, he developed a rationale for reconciling wider participation with enhanced state power in a manner quite congenial to older Chinese constitutional thinking. Wei Yuan's lifelong meditation on the relationships between activism and loyalism, between moral rectitude and practical politics, remained within the framework of the classical canon; yet it demonstrates how the manifold meanings of that canon could be reintegrated in new ways to address the special dilemmas of the late-imperial age.

Chapter 2 explores the problem of whether the public interest can be reconciled with political competition (the "faction" problem) by examining how some ordinary bureaucrats (and a few extraordinary ones) reacted to the unorthodox proposals of the late reformer Feng Guifen. Their reactions, in the atmosphere of the Reform Movement of 1898, expose the prevailing suspicion of political competition and suggest some of its underlying sources. Whether the clash of private interests can ever be compatible with the preservation of the public interest, a question near the top of the constitutional agenda in today's China, used to be a matter of lively debate in the West; this chapter ends with some historical reflections on how the issue was phrased in the early years of the American republic.

Chapter 3 addresses the decreasing ability of local administration to govern China's huge, complex rural society: specifically, the state's unending struggle to garner the agricultural surplus without allowing it to disappear into the pockets of middlemen along the way. The story of a tax-rebellion in the mid-nineteenth century illustrates the anarchy that the Qing tax system generated at the county level. With this scene as backdrop, we explore how one resort of the modern state—agricultural collectivization—was designed in large part to address this longstanding dilemma of Chinese statecraft. In the context of the transformative vision of the Communist Party in the 1950s and 1960s, collectivization seemed a plausible way to solve the state's fiscal problems—but, as it turned out, at ruinous cost.

Chapter 4 traces how the terms of the old agenda were transformed over the course of the nineteenth and twentieth centuries, as constitutional thinkers sought to save China from foreign domination. In this process, the old relationships between participation and authority, between public interest and private interests, and between state and communities, were addressed in the new vocabularies of nationalism and citizenship. Even as the established literati were putting themselves forward as a transitional group on the way toward a modern citizenry, they were quickly superseded by broader social groups, who engaged in new forms of community activism in a spirit of national commitment. Though the old agenda was reworded and updated, its most basic constitutional tensions nevertheless were unresolved, and remain so to this day. These tensions form the underlying subject matter of politics in the ongoing quest for a state that meets the needs of the Chinese people.

CHAPTER I

Participation and Authority in the Thought of Wei Yuan

Wei Yuan (1794–1857) was arguably the most influential political thinker of his age. What the political philosopher and activist Liang Qichao was to the twentieth century, Wei Yuan, *mutatis mutandis*, was to the nineteenth. Inasmuch as his views were shared by many contemporary political activists, I regard Wei (like Liang) as emblematic of a trend of thought, one that was to have major consequences for China's modern history.[1] Here I shall explore a strand of his thinking—the relationship between participation and authority—that bears upon the constitutional development of the modern state.

A persistent theme of Wei's political writing is the legitimate boundary of the national polity: defining that part of the community that properly participates in national politics. In China, drawing this boundary has been compli-

---

[1]For the breadth of Wei's influence, see Li Borong, *Wei Yuan shiyu ji* (Changsha: Hunan daxue chubanshe, 1983). Also Li Hanwu, *Wei Yuan zhuan* (Changsha: Yuelushe, 1988), 248–83. Wei's influence spread through his network of friends and colleagues and not, of course, through the public press as in Liang's case.

cated by the fact that literacy (or more properly, in imperial China, literati status) is much more widely distributed than political power. This is of course a condition not limited to China. But the special poignancy of this issue in China, since the beginning of imperial times, is that the literati were trained to consider politics their special vocation. And I would argue that the political vocation of the Chinese elite has traditionally included a general interest in *national* politics, particularly in the quality and legitimacy of government.

Yet the narrowness of the imperial bureaucracy ensured that only a tiny fraction of literati could actually participate in government at any level. Here was the irony of the Chinese educational system: at least one component of elite education, that which dealt with the interests of the nation and the historical-theoretical basis of legitimate national rule, was training men to be concerned about issues which the state was determined to keep most of them out of. Men in office and men out of office shared a common literati status, but their actual power was grossly unequal. One might rationalize one's exclusion from power by sanctimonious, fastidious objections to serving in a corrupt or illegitimate regime. Yet when the state was menaced by foreign invaders and domestic rebels, as it was in the nineteenth and twentieth centuries, it became harder to resign oneself to the role of bystander.

Did the breadth of the polity affect the powers of the state? The liberal historian will assume that broader participation might imply certain restraints on the central power-holders, including the throne. Indeed, in the imperial system of Wei Yuan's day, a suitable balance between arbitrary power and bureaucratic routine was essential to the secure pursuit of official careers. The coercive power of the state, moreover, could not be exercised so capriciously or so ruthlessly as to damage the social system upon which literati careers depended. How much the more would restraints be required in a more broadly based polity! Wei Yuan's times, however, were ill-suited to the moderate and temporizing literati style; instead they seemed to require a state more militant toward foreign enemies, and bloodier toward domestic. How did Wei and his contemporaries perceive the relationship between enhanced state power and the breadth of the polity? The character of this relationship, as revealed in his political writings, suggests how the origins of China's modern state were connected to the constitutional issues of the late empire.

There are several excellent studies of Wei's life and thought.[2] Here, I should like to consider only those aspects of his biography that are directly relevant to our present subject. Wei's background had immersed him personally in China's social crisis. Born to a family of small landowners and traders on the margins of the local elite, Wei experienced directly the economic effects of social disorder (the West China rebellions of the 1790s), and witnessed the im-

---

[2] Biographies include Wang Jiajian, *Wei Yuan nianpu* (Taipei: Jinghua, 1967); Huang Liyong, *Wei Yuan nianpu* (Changsha: Hunan renmin chubanshe, 1985); and Li Hanwu, *Wei Yuan zhuan*. Analyses of his thought that I have found most helpful are Liu Guangjing (Kwang-ching Liu), "Shijiu shiji chuye Zhongguo zhishi fenzi—Bao Shichen yu Wei Yuan," *Zhongyang yanjiuyuan guoji Hanxue huiyi lunwenji* (Taibei, 1981), 995–1030; Chen Yaonan (Chan Yiu-nam), *Wei Yuan yanjiu* (Hong Kong: Zhaoming, 1979); and Qi Sihe, "Wei Yuan yu wan Qing xuefeng," *Yanjing xuebao* 39 (Dec. 1950), 177–226; and most recently, He Guangru (Ho Goang-ru), *Wei Moshen sixiang tanjiu: yi chuantong jingdian de quanshuo wei taolun zhongxin* (Taipei: Guoli Taiwan daxue, 1999). In English see Jane Kate Leonard, *Wei Yuan and China's Rediscovery of the Maritime World* (Cambridge, Mass.: Council on East Asian Studies, Harvard University, 1984).

pact of state power on local society. He was also keenly aware, at every milestone of his own youth, of major threats to the established order.[3] Wei's theoretical writings on politics were thus firmly rooted in the grim realities of rural life and in the recurrent crises of a weakening state.

His political career illustrates the political ambiguity embedded in China's social order: between men in office and men out of office, the gradient of power was very steep; yet the gradient of social status was not. Wei himself held no administrative rank until late in life and served less than a year in a minor office.[4] Yet he was deeply engaged in the factional politics of the 1820s and 1830s under the protection of official patrons. These patrons, high-placed provincial leaders, were bound to him by shared literati culture and densely woven personal ties. It was this ambiguity in the status system that permitted the state to absorb, on its margins, talents such as Wei's. But it also raised the awkward question of how such political participation might be given an acceptable rationale, by which the mass of out-of-office literati could participate more actively in national politics. This question, central to Wei's

[3]In his preface to the *Shengwu ji* (History of military campaigns of the Qing), Wei notes that he was born the year preceding the revolt and suppression of the Miao aborigines in 1795; that his student years coincided with the government suppression of the White Lotus rebellion and the coastal pirates; and that he attained his first advanced degree (*bagongsheng*) in 1813, the year of the Eight Trigrams rebellion. Qi Sihe, "Wei Yuan yu wan Qing xuefeng," pp. 178–79.

[4]Wei received his first appointment in 1845 (the year he attained the doctorate) as magistrate of Dongtai xian, Jiangsu, a post he had to vacate the following year because of his mother's death. Three years later he was appointed magistrate of Xinghua xian, Jiangsu; and subsequently, to his ultimate posting (1850–53) as department magistrate (*zhizhou*) of Gaoyou, Jiangsu (rank: 5a). He was discharged in 1853 after being impeached by a political enemy. Wang Jiajian, *Wei Yuan nianpu*, pp. 142, 147, 158, 182–83.

concerns, became more urgent as China slipped deeper into her modern crisis.

To Westerners, Wei Yuan has been an appealing figure, but for somewhat ethnocentric reasons. As the author of China's first systematic treatise on the Western nations (a work of strategic intelligence compiled on the basis of information assembled during the Opium War), Wei has been considered by Westerners as "progressive" in his outward-looking realism. As compiler of an immense collection of source materials on "statecraft," he has been praised as a practical-minded activist in an age of *mandarins fainéants*. As a believer in the irreversibility of history, Wei has been considered a forerunner of unilinear thinking pleasing to Westerners, whether liberal or Marxist. I suggest, however, that Wei's importance for our understanding of the modern Chinese state lies elsewhere.

To generalize the experience and the ambitions of his own social group, to give his particular worldview a universal significance, is the talent of a constitutional thinker. Wei's ambiguous position, closely tied to circles of great power yet never personally in command of such power, was shared by many literati of his age. It was his special role to distill, from such circumstances, a general significance and to express it in a universalistic rhetoric. Wei's constitutional writing is notable for its lack of attention to concrete programs for political change. This may seem strange in a statesman who was renowned for his specific proposals about institutions such as the salt monopoly and the Grain Transport Administration. In matters of deeper constitutional import, however, the practical mechanics of change seem of secondary importance to him. Indeed, in his skepticism about the ability of legislation to influence human behavior, his writing would have been more agreeable to Burke than to Condorcet. Programs for changing the constitutional order would await Wei's successors. But Wei raised the main issue: how the state could be invigorated by more fervent commitment and broader political participation among the literati elite, and at the same time be strengthened in the exercise of its authoritarian rule. This seems a conundrum to us, but (I shall suggest) was not one for Wei Yuan.

Wei's constitutional thought drew its force from his realization that his own age was unique in Chinese history. He wrote, on the eve of the Opium War:

> Not a year has passed without fears of Yellow River floods, not a year without having to raise funds for river control. This is something unknown in previous ages. Foreign opium has spread throughout the country, and silver flows overseas. Because of this the grain-tribute tax and salt monopoly develop ever more evils, the officials and people are ever deeper in trouble. This too is something unknown in former ages . . . This is why, though our dynasty matches the Three Ages [of antiquity] in its frugality and benevolence, disasters in the empire often exceed what we are prepared for. Standing in the present and surveying the past, the difference is as between black and white.[5]

What had happened? China had passed through a century of unprecedented population growth and its ecological consequence—the fateful siltation of riverbeds by erosion of overcultivated hillsides. Added now was the foreign disaster: by the 1820s, the domestic economy was unsettled by

troubles

[5]"Mingdai shibing erzhenglu xu," *Wei Yuan Ji* (Beijing: Zhonghua shuju, 1976), p. 163. Cited hereafter as WYJ. In this passage Wei also complains about the fecklessness of the literati of his day, which was also "unknown in earlier ages."

currency disorders, caused partly by a worldwide silver shortage and partly by the outflow of silver in payment for ~~breakdown~~ opium. This economic crisis had already touched off widespread rural rebellion, which now became a perennial theme in national affairs. Accordingly, the early decades of the nineteenth century found the ruling dynasty in serious trouble. The prestige of the throne had been eroded by corruption scandals, its orthodox cosmology and its local control challenged by heterodox religious sects, its competence cast in doubt by the breakdown of the flood-control system. In such circumstances, one resource that a conquest dynasty could ill afford to neglect was its legitimacy in the eyes of the cultural elite.

But the dynasty was not well situated to rally support from that elite. It was a regime tightly controlled by high-ranking insiders. During the reigns of the eighteenth-century monarchs Yongzheng and Qianlong, political combinations of literati had been condemned as factions and punished resolutely. Accordingly, even the crises of the early nineteenth century prompted no abrupt change in literati behavior. Such a change would have required the elite to overcome their deeply rooted political timidity, their scholastic apathy, and particularly their well-founded fear of coming together in support of a common agenda. A rationale for just such a change forms the central thread of Wei Yuan's constitutional writings.

These writings were assembled in his *Treatise on Scholarship and Government* (*Mogu*), thirty essays that got pride of place in his collected works.[6] Wei's credibility, like that of

<hr>

[6]What I refer to here awkwardly as "*Treatise* . . . ," Wei gave the allusive title *Mogu*. On one level, this simply means "Wei Yuan's writing-tablet": *Mo* being a component of Wei's courtesy name, and *gu* being a sort of wooden writing-tablet

many political figures of his age, rested upon his accomplishments as a classical scholar. He anchored his argumentation in his studies of *The Book of Odes* (*Shijing*), a collection of ancient poetry that had become an orthodox text at the royal court by the sixth century BCE. By the time of Confucius, the *Odes* were a reference point for discussions of moral conduct and social practice, as well as a safe way to criticize the powerful by allusion.[7]

Wei Yuan's "Preface" to his major study of the *Odes* (*Shiguwei*, or Ancient subtleties of the Odes) shows why he considered them so relevant to constitutional issues. The *Odes*, he believed, were not to be understood (in the manner of the dominant "Mao Commentary") as having referred originally to particular persons or events of antiquity, in the conventional "praise and blame" mode of explication. Instead, Wei accorded them a significance more general (we would say, "constitutional"): in them could be found guidance for the public life of the present age. This guidance could be discerned in the *Odes* as the superior moral and political insights of antiquity, including those of

used in antiquity. But *mo* may also allude to a phrase in the *Analects* (7:2): "*mo er shi zhi*" (listening silently and storing up knowledge); and *gu* to a phrase in *Jijiu pian*, a Han pedagogical text: *qigu yu zhong yi*, "an unconventional [work written on a] wooden tablet" (*Qinding siku quanshu*, Taipei: Taiwan shangwu yinshuguan, 1983, 223:4). My thanks to Ch'en Hsi-yuan for these suggestions. Although the *Mogu* is undated, He Guangru has shown that the material in it dates from various times between 1824 and 1855, and originally represented Wei's reflections on his reading during most of his adult life. She believes it possible that Wei gave the work a final editing toward the end of his life, yet concludes that it may serve as a guide to the development of his thought over a long span of years. He, *Wei Moshen*, pp. 237–57. The work comprises "Essays on Scholarship" (*xuepian*) and "Essays on Governance" (*zhipian*). Originally published as part of Wei's *Guweitang neiji* (1878), it is reprinted in WYJ. I am grateful to Lu Baoqian, of the Institute of Modern History, Academia Sinca, for guiding me in my study of *Mogu*.

[7]On this subject see François Martin, "Le *Shijing*, de la citation à l'allusion: la disponibilité du sens," *Extrême-Orient Extrême-Occident* 17 (1995), pp. 11–39.

the anonymous poets, and of the *Odes*' supposed editor, Confucius himself. Here Wei was following the "modern text" tradition, a minor interpretive school dating from the mid-second century BCE.[8] In brief, this tradition of textual commentary attributed to the Confucian classics a prophetic intent to influence mankind's future, through the cryptic expression of "great meanings in subtle language." To return to the "modern text" understanding of the *Odes*, Wei maintained, "would reveal how the Duke of Zhou and Confucius showed their concern for future generations."[9] In this way the *Odes* could resume their rightful role as

[8]A somewhat eccentric approach to the Classics had developed among scholars in the city of Changzhou, in the lower Yangzi, around 1770: a kind of scholarly research that rested on "modern texts" or *jinwen* (literally, texts in "modern" script—modern, that is, for the Han era) and their commentaries, which had been in vogue during the Former Han Dynasty (206 BCE–8 CE). The "ancient text" versions of the Classics (*guwen*), written in an archaic script, served as the orthodox canon in the late empires and the basis for the imperial examination system. These "ancient" texts had allegedly been "discovered" in a cache buried in a wall of Confucius's old house. Their supposed antiquity gave them the authority needed to displace the "modern text" versions. With only a few surviving writings of the modern text school, the Changzhou scholars undertook to legitimate them as a standard commentary on the *Spring and Autumn Annals* (*Chunqiu*), a revered text supposedly edited by Confucius. For a concise account, see Benjamin Elman, *Classicism, Politics, and Kinship: The Ch'ang-chou School of New Text Confucianism in Late Imperial China* (Berkeley: University of California Press, 1990), pp. xxi-xxx. See also Anne Cheng, "Tradition canonique et ésprit réformiste à la fin du XIXe siècle en Chine: la résurgence de la controverse *jinwen/guwen* sous les Qing," *Études Chinoises* 14.2 (1995), pp. 7–42. For comparison, imagine that in the fourth century CE, rabbinical scholars claimed to have discovered, in a Jerusalem cellar, a collection of texts written in ancient Hebrew, in which Jesus appeared as a learned rabbi seeking to revive morality and basing himself on ancient Judaic Law (like the Confucius of the "ancient text" classics), and not as a divine prophet; and that this new interpretation, rather than the gospels of the Evangelists, was proclaimed the orthodox canon of the Roman Empire!

[9]On Wei's study of the *Shijing*, see Chen Yaonan, Li Hanwu, and Tang Zhijun, "Wei Yuan di 'bianyi' sixiang he *Shi*, *Shu* guwei," in Yang Shenzhi and Huang Liyong, eds., *Wei Yuan sixiang yanjiu* (Hunan: Renmin chubanshe, 1987), 170–90. He Guangru, *Wei Moshen*, pp. 97–162.

"writings of remonstrance" (*jianshu*), both to rulers and to society at large.[10]

In Wei's view, the *Odes* reached beyond the fleeting issues of day-to-day politics to the very character of public life: they were material for a rhetoric that we may justly call "constitutional." Wei's departure from a more narrowly text-based scholarship on the *Odes* earned him some reproach for interpretations that went well beyond the evidence. By the standards of the "empirical research" school of his day, such reproaches were certainly justified. Yet for Wei, scholarship was not a mere academic exercise, but a guide to action.[11] The *Book of Odes* was not an antique bronze bell to be authenticated and fondled, but a tocsin in the night!

By using exegesis of the *Odes* as a vehicle for political commentary, Wei was writing within a well-established tradition. His Ancient subtleties assembled *Odes*-inspired essays from a number of authors, including, among others, his scholarly icon Gu Yanwu (1613–82), progenitor of the school of empirical research; the modern-text scholar Zhuang Cunyu (1719–88); and the classicist and Ming loyalist, Wang Fuzhi (1619–92). Although all these writers had used *Odes* passages freely to illustrate their own social and

---

[10]Such a broad interpretation of the *Odes*' purposes had been common in the early days of the empire (Western Han), when Confucians at court evidently had used the *Odes*, along with omens and portents, to exercise some degree of control over headstrong monarchs. Yet even in those days, scholars of the ancient text school were beginning to adopt a more modest sort of *Odes* interpretation, which eschewed overambitious interpretations in favor of a narrowly annotative scholarship linking particular *Odes* to specific persons or events of high antiquity. See Chen Yaonan et al., p. 73; also Steven Jay Van Zoeren, *Poetry and Personality: Reading, Exegesis, and Hermeneutics in Traditional China* (Stanford, Calif.: Stanford University Press, 1991), pp. 83–84.

[11]Chen Yaonan et al., p. 79.

historical ideas, Wei Yuan's own interpretation of the *Odes* was more ambitious in its use of the text for political rhetoric.

In using the *Odes* to epitomize general truths about public life, Wei evidently had in mind the philosopher Xunzi (third century BCE), who had appended stanzas of the *Odes* as pithy, allusive epigraphs to sum up sections of an exposition (just as Wei used them himself); and also the only extant "modern text" treatment of the *Odes*, Han Ying's *Exoteric Commentary* (second century BCE).[12] Wei also acknowledged his debt to the ancient poet Qu Yuan, who had written in the allusive tradition of the *Odes* to comment on great principles: "Using beneficent birds and fragrant herbs to signify loyalty and uprightness; fearsome beasts and filthy things to symbolize slander and villainy." Wei was intent upon discovering the "poets' intention," which had more profound and more general significance than the intention of those who later cited or collected the *Odes* for their own rhetorical purposes.[13] The *Odes*, insisted Wei, could never have originated as mere occasion pieces, to "praise or blame" particular persons or actions (as the orthodox commentary would have it), but "were written

[handwritten margin note: Comment on great principles]

[12]*The Exoteric Commentary on Han's Odes* (*Hanshi waizhuan*—second century BCE) was the only surviving *Odes* commentary associated with the modern text school. See James R. Hightower, *Han Shih Wai Chuan: Han Ying's Illustrations of the Didactic Application of the Classic of Songs* (Cambridge, Mass.: Harvard University Press, 1952). It was Wei Yuan's intention, in his *Shiguwei*, to revive the "great meanings expressed in subtle words" embedded in this commentary, and in the two other modern text commentaries (the "Qi" and the "Lu"), which survived only in fragments (Qi and Lu were two principalities in Shandong, the home province of Confucius). Wei saw these alternative traditions as necessary counterparts to the orthodox "Mao" commentary—a syncretic approach that cannot rigidly be called "modern text." He simply believed that it was necessary to go beyond the "Mao" to reach the *Odes'* deeper meanings. See Li Hanwu, pp. 221–22.

[13]Chen Yaonan et al., "Wei Yuan di 'bianyi' sixiang . . . ," pp. 185–86.

by benevolent sages to express their most ardent concerns."[14]

The *Odes* and their music were composed in order to promulgate the sovereign's virtue and to transmit the feelings of the people. By guiding grief and happiness, by producing loyalty and filiality, they are the constant complement of public affairs. Therefore by disseminating them in both village and nation, men's hearts will be moved and the realm will be at peace."[15]

The phonological and historical exegesis so prized by eighteenth-century scholars, Wei believed, had actually alienated people from the meaning of the classics, particularly the *Odes*. The more transcendant significance of the *Odes*, the "hidden meanings," would change the consciousness of a decadent and apathetic elite. But exactly how were these "hidden meanings" to affect men's minds?

When the soundless Rites and Music and the noble aspirations [of the Sages] are stifled in Heaven and Earth, this is when the functions of "incitement to moral awareness (*xing*)," "critical observation [of men's characters] (*guan*)," "sociability (*qun*)," and "expression of just grievances (*yuan*)" are exercised by the *Odes*. And [these functions rely] not just on the [conventional] chapter-and-sentence explication of the *Odes*.[16]

The four functions Wei refers to were attributed to Confucius himself, who was explaining to his disciples why they should study the *Odes*.[17] Their meaning in Confucius's day must have expressed the identity of his own class of

[14]WYJ, pp. 231–32. Quoted in Chen Yaonan et al., p. 62.
[15]WYJ, pp. 244–45. Quoted in Chen Yaonan et al., p. 62. Both Xunzi and Qu Yuan had been associated with the Kingdom of Chu, the ancient region with which Wei, as a Hunanese, identified himself.
[16]WYJ, p. 120.
[17]*Analects* 17.9.

lower-level elite, for whom the *Odes* were becoming a necessary part of a gentleman's cultural equipment. The language of the *Odes*, well memorized, could shape one's inward social feelings and give elegant form to one's outward expression. When we examine the references to these functions in the *Analects* of Confucius, it seems that none of them had a specifically political connotation. "Sociability," for instance, Confucius explicitly distinguished from "forming factions" (*dang*). It probably meant a capacity to associate, with proper deportment, with men of one's own social stratum. But we may well wonder whether "sociability" served Wei Yuan as a decorous cloak for political activism. By the early twentieth century, *qun* in the writings of Liang Qichao was used in a similar sense: activism in the public interest, free of the taint of faction.

But it is clear, at least, that Wei regarded the *Odes* as more than an elegant cultural template. Instead, they were to provide a galvanizing force for the elite of a decadent age: they would move the literati from apathy to public commitment; from social fragmentation to greater awareness of common identity and interests; and from prudent silence to forthright expression of opinion.

Wei's examination of the question "What are the legitimate boundaries of the polity" exemplifies his rhetorical use of the *Odes*. He begins from the assertion that truth, in politics, assumes multiple appearances (at least, the contingent truth of our mundane affairs): "There is no single doctrine which is absolutely correct, and no single person who is absolutely good. That is why, in the Ode 'Deer Call,' the deer cry out to each other when foraging for food."[18] The

---

[18]WYJ, p. 35.

poem to which Wei refers is conventionally understood to
read, "The deer cry out to one another while grazing on the
watercress in the field. I have excellent guests; for them the
lute is struck and the flute played. . . . They love me, they
will teach me the Great Way (the principles of wisdom)."[19]
Wei knows that his readers have been accustomed to associate the poem with a harmonious relationship between a
ruler and his ministers (who are symbolized by the deer).[20]
Yet in Wei's treatment of the Ode, what stands out is *the
communication among the deer*. If correct policies are to
emerge through discussion, not flow downward from a
single source; the elite must overcome its fear of intercom-
munication in public affairs, of seeming to organize factions. At the same time, the monarch must accord such
consultation the legitimacy that had been denied it by four
generations of rulers since the Manchu conquest of China.

From the Forbidden City down to provincial capitals, a
broad search for policy opinion must replace dictation by
insiders operating from back rooms. "Reading the Ode,
'Brilliant Are the Flowers,' one exclaims with a sigh, 'How
well the author of this Ode understood the governance of
the realm!'" The first stanza reads, "I shall seek everywhere
for information and advice . . ."[21]

How might one explain why men of great personal recti-

[19]Translated from Séraphin Couvreur, S.J., *Cheu King*, 3rd ed. (Sien-hien, Imprimerie de la Mission Catholique, 1934), p. 174. Arthur Waley considered Couvreur's to be the best translation based on the traditional Neo-Confucian interpretation by Zhu Xi.
[20]Zhu Xi, whose twelfth-century commentaries were the reigning orthodoxy in
Qing times, wrote that this Ode exemplified "the sincerity of mutual liking between
guest and host." *Zhuzi yulei* (Taipei: Huashi, 1987), p. 2117.
[21]WYJ, p.35; Couvreur, pp. 177–78.

tude could still be political failures? Their fatal flaw was an exaggerated faith in their own political self-sufficiency.

Taking the empty theory of "sitting in place with a correct bearing" and applying it to practical affairs will be effective less than three or four times out of ten. If one takes one's individual ideas and checks them with people here and there, there will be agreement in only five or six cases out of ten.[22]

Referring obliquely to the conquest dynasty under which he himself was living, Wei pointed out how an ancient conqueror, the Duke of Zhou, established the legitimacy of the Zhou Dynasty by consulting eminent scholars throughout the realm of the conquered Shang kings. To establish dynastic legitimacy, "Gaining the hearts of the scholars" was the conqueror's first task. "Would not the hearts of the common people follow?"[23]

Assuming, then, that powerholders should seek broadly for different views, whose views should they seek? Wei Yuan was quite sure that the common people had no appropriate role in politics, save as objects of rule, and in this opinion he was entirely conventional. But scholars (*shi*) — that is, literati who were not office-holders — were a different matter.

Exactly who was to be included in that category? Wei assuredly did not include those lower elite who had obtained only the first degree, the "students" (*shengyuan*), mostly rural or small-town residents, who were not even eligible for official appointment. The countryside, Wei assures us, is not a natural habitat for scholars. "When the sage kings sought scholars, and scholars sought The Way, it

[22]WYJ, p. 35.
[23]WYJ, pp. 58–59.

was definitely not in rustic places, but in walled administrative cities." There, "people are densely gathered, so a lively spirit is also dense; and a lively spirit means a gathering-place for talent." Indeed, the countryside may be quite hostile to learning.

The air of the mountains and woods is pure, but there are no Rites and Music, no teachers and friends for support. If a city scholar whose education is not complete goes into the mountains, then he is abandoning the bright and luminous for the confined and shadowed. Thus a young lower-degree holder should stay in the [provincial] capital, and discussions of ideas should take place in the provincial academies.

If there should be a lower-degree holder who is talented enough to stand out in his rustic abode, he should be brought to the city, where the provincial grandees can patronize and encourage him. Powerful patrons would never prefer a rural scholar to one whose urban connections and education made him part of the national elite. As the Ode reads, "From the floor of the valley, [the birds] fly to the tops of the great trees."[24]

Despite his rural origins, Wei's years in the provincial capital, and later in Beijing, had made him a man of the city; his scorn for the "rustic" lower-degree holders was entirely conventional for his era and social class. Although China was even less urbanized in the nineteenth century than it had been a millenium earlier, the idea that urban elites should control rural bumpkins still dominated Chinese political theory.[25]

By "scholars," Wei, not surprisingly, meant men like

[24]WYJ, p. 62; Couvreur, p. 180.
[25]On the urbanization rate, see G. William Skinner, ed., *The City in Late Imperial China*, pp. 28–29.

himself: urban literati eligible for official appointment, but not actually holding office (Wei once modestly used the term "lowly scholar" (*xiashi*) in reference to himself. He was then aged 32, a holder of the provincial civil-service degree, and already a staff adviser (*muyou*) of high officials.)[26] Wei Yuan's views on the proper scope of the polity seem well suited to an age when the supply of highly educated men had grossly outrun the political system's capacity to absorb their energies and ideas. This group, whose participation Wei was promoting, let us call "established literati," to distinguish them from the much larger, lower-ranking group of first-degree holders (*shengyuan*), whom Wei distrusted. "Established literati" were probably coterminous in his mind with *juren* like himself—provincial graduates who constituted a *de facto* national (but non-official) elite.

Gaining the allegiance of established literati was, however, no ritual exercise. Wei Yuan insisted that the establishment of correct government policies required actual competition among men of varying views. The presumption that political truth emerges through the clash of varied opinions is indeed one well-known justification offered for the encouragement of freedom of speech in the West—and one that does not rely upon a theory of natural rights. Although Wei Yuan is certainly not reaching here for a rationale for "freedom of speech," he implies strongly that competition between ideas can result in more effective decision-making by the autocrat. "When sagacious officials are at court, their views do not necessarily coincide. But when the sovereign uses two views to reach one, their views

[26]WYJ, p. 398. Wei notes that, once he had "achieved eligibility for office" (*zhongliu*) by gaining the *juren* degree, he was considered qualified to take up a staff position as *muyou* and to draft policy papers on public questions.

invariably shine in succession, and he can choose one to implement." The perfect staff-man's point of view! However, Wei goes on to suggest a more general skepticism about our ability to reach absolute political truth. As the Ode says, "The turbid water of the River Jing seems even murkier when one sees it flowing alongside the limpid water of the River Wei. However, it flows clear near the little islets [where the current is slower]."[27] This Ode was conventionally explicated to deplore the injustice of the king's judging an old wife by comparison to a younger, prettier one. Wei gives it a more general significance: we can grasp political truth only in the light of comparison and context.

The problem of long-entrenched powerholders is, of course, a problem that concerns any outsider. Rigid policies produce frozen patronage—not a good political environment for men on the margins of politics. Wei shared the modern text vision of a heroic style of political leadership—like that of Confucius, himself, in modern text tradition—and believed that such heroic leadership was needed in periods of national emergency. Such a messianic view meant, to Wei, that routine functionaries, or "able officials" (*nengchen*), were entirely unsuitable political leaders in an age of desperate peril (which he knew his own age to be). What was needed, instead, were "gifted officials" (*caichen*), men of large vision and stern resolution.[28] Among such men he surely must have counted his political intimate and patron, Lin Zexu (1785–1850), leader of the radical anti-opium faction that precipitated the Opium War. The churning effect of replacing conventional bureaucrats with heroic leaders

[27]WYJ, p. 50; Couvreur, p. 40.
[28]WYJ, p. 54.

could, in another context, have had a revolutionary outcome. Wei had in mind, certainly not revolution, but rather a more dynamic and powerful central state, one that could deal more effectively with its domestic and foreign troubles. (That such a vision of leadership was not confined to modern text scholars was shortly to be demonstrated by Zeng Guofan, the scholar-general who rescued the dynasty from internal rebellion, and who was firmly in the ancient text tradition.)

For his part, the scholar's responsibility was to prepare himself for public service. But Wei considered the civil-service examination system to be worse than useless (he himself only attained the metropolitan degree at the age of fifty). How can the perils of the present age "be handled effectively by scholars who have come up through the hack schoolroom texts of the examination system?" Instead, the scholar should cultivate a relentless inquisitiveness about practical affairs.

Suppose your utterances all concern "mind and nature," and one's personal demeanor all "ceremonies and righteousness"; . . . but if you do not examine the people's ills, do not study administration, do not look into the state's revenues and border defenses: then supposing one day you enter official service. You will be unable to manage state revenues, unable to pacify the borders, and unable to relieve the people's troubles![29]

Entrusted by his patron, the reformist provincial official He Changling (1785–1848) to edit a large collection of materials on government, Wei published in 1826 the *Collected Essays on Statecraft*, which was designed to encourage broader interest by scholars in practical questions such as these. De-

[29]WYJ, p. 36.

spite its reliance on the writings of establishment elites, there seems, in retrospect, something a bit risky about this publication, from the standpoint of the imperial system as it then existed. What good could possibly result from this invitation to inquisitiveness, this suggestion that questions of high policy were the proper business of men outside government?

Such an appeal for involvement of established literati in politics could never have occurred without the patronage of high-placed officials. We know that such prominent provincial figures as He Changling, Tao Shu (1779–1839) and Lin Zexu, all prominent officials in the lower Yangzi region, the fiscal core of the empire, were seeking to break the power of such bureaucratic leviathans as the salt monopoly and the Grain Transport Administration, whose territorial power cut across that of provincial governors and whose rapacity was ruining local communities. Small wonder that these officials were mobilizing literati suport outside bureaucratic channels, and that Wei's project had their backing! Such a strategy, already a fact in the 1820s, was a precursor of the mobilization of literati outrage over the opium question a decade later.[30] In both contexts, government repression of nonofficial literati activism was shown to have lost its force; and to have given place to a selective encouragement of literati political engagement.

〜

By this point in our discussion, nobody could be faulted for conceiving a possible connection between the sort of broader literati participation that Wei envisaged and a tran-

[30]James Polachek, *The Inner Opium War* (Cambridge, Mass.: Council on East Asian Studies, Harvard University, 1992), offers detailed confirmation of this point.

sition to some form of civil society, which would eventuate in greater diffusion of political power in society at large. Here, however, is exactly where we can discern the power of China's own political agenda.

Two centuries of state-building under the Qing conquerors had refined the machinery of centralized monarchy to a point not seen before in Chinese history. The problem with this monarchy, from the viewpoint of Wei Yuan, was that it was run by too few hands, and not necessarily the best ones; that its narrow circles of power were increasingly ignorant of the nation's problems; that its enmity to factions had so weakened elite backbones as to make possible the virtual takeover of the monarchy by a single faction (that of Heshen).

During those two centuries, the literati had witnessed social changes that made the centralized state more important to them than ever. Because their social position rested upon no inherited status system, their elite identity and their local interests could, ultimately, be protected by no power but that of the state. Their families' economic prospects depended upon obtaining academic degrees and administrative posts that only the state could provide. The tripling of China's population under Qing rule and the resulting danger to social stability left the elite particularly vulnerable. It was a time not for weakening authoritarian rule, but for strengthening it. This last point was to emerge insistently as Western aggression made nationalism the central theme of elite politics during the dynasty's last years.

Wei Yuan maintained, as we have seen, an entirely conventional view of the basic division between an enlightened urban elite and a docile rural mass (a view, as we shall see in the third of these essays, that has survived to the present day). The view that the urbanized, established literati should be more broadly included in the governing elite was accompanied by no suggestion of a more general theory of political inclusiveness. As we might expect, Wei's was far from a general theory based on innate rights. Instead, the rationale for broader participation was not justice, but governmental effectiveness.

From a Western perspective, here lies the distinctiveness of the Chinese case: Wei repeatedly associated broader participation not with limiting state power, but with enhancing it. As an example, consider his summons to the literati to put aside their supposedly principled distaste for practical government.

To energize the established literati's political vocation required Wei to confront their well-founded timidity (long fostered by the Manchu conquerors), as well as a certain moral fastidiousness, among some literati, about administrative service. Such fastidiousness could be expressed either as exclusive devotion to the joys of pure scholarship, or as a concern that the "Kingly Way" (*wangdao*, or government by moral example) was impossible in the real world. Wei's argument went directly to the relationship between means and ends. The practical techniques of government—whether in agriculture, taxation, defense, or law—were (he maintained) actually close to the hearts of the culture-heroes of antiquity.

As soon as King Yu had pacified the waters and land, he instituted the tribute and taxes; and bent his efforts to military defense. . . . A sufficiency of food and of military power served as tools for governing the empire.[31]

[31]WYJ, p. 36.

Where, then, had his own literati colleagues derived such disdain for practical administration? It was, Wei concluded, a misunderstanding. Confucius's most prominent disciple, Mencius, had stressed that the primary instrument of rule was the ruler's moral conduct, the mark of the "True King" or "Kingly Way." By contrast, the "Five Hegemons" of late antiquity (military strongmen of lesser virtue) exemplified raw power and weak legitimacy. Literati of later ages had relied on this distinction, Wei wrote, to accord moral qualities greater value than practical governing skills. As a result, Wei believed, "they regarded military strength and food supply as concerns only of the Five Hegemons."[32]

But, insisted Wei, the Kingly Way "is finely textured and all-encompassing. Through it runs all the pure and subtle quiddity of existence, including farming and herding, corvée management, military and fiscal affairs." Indeed, "From ancient times, there have been wealth and power (*fuqiang*) that were exercised apart from the Kingly Way, but never the Kingly Way exercised apart from wealth and power."[33] By "wealth and power," Wei means that of the state, not of individuals; the expression is exactly the one proclaimed by the "self-strengthening" statesmen of the late nineteenth century, as they set about importing Western technology to strengthen the moribund Qing regime.

Is the distinction between True King and Hegemon, then, meaningless? Wei confronts this question without flinching: "The distinction between True King and Hegemon lies in their intentions, but not in their actions. Their intentions are characterized, respectively, by princi-

[32]Ibid.
[33]Ibid.

ples of public good and private good; but their actions are not greatly different."[34]

Wei's immediate point is that the grubby business of civil and military affairs will not sap the scholars' moral integrity, assuming that they have any. The more general implication, however, is that authoritarian government, with its armies, its courts, and its tax collectors, must be judged by its ends, not its means. For rigor and ruthlessness, the well-intentioned ruler cannot be condemned.

Shall we then consider Wei as an advocate of remorseless *realpolitik*, a believer that men's evil nature is best controlled by "rewards and punishments," in the manner of the ancient Legalists (*fajia*)? I see him, rather, as closer to the mainstream of imperial Confucianism, which drew selectively from the Legalist tradition. Rewards and punishments had their place, but mainly for the unenlightened commoners: "Punishments to deter evil conduct are for the commoners; commands to deter willful conduct are for the officials, and ceremonies to protect virtue are the way for the sages and worthy men to govern themselves."[35]

Furthermore, the power of government had natural limits. "Laws that force men to do what they cannot do, cannot stand; laws that forbid what men must do, cannot be carried out." And nothing but disruption could result from imposing sudden, radical change by legal fiat.[36] Wei was born into the relative sanity of the premodern age: government could not hope to achieve a fundamental transformation of human nature. Considering China's present-day hybrid system of authoritarian politics and entrepreneurial

[34]Ibid.
[35]Ibid., p. 45.
[36]Ibid.

economics ("market socialism"), it is worth our notice that Wei Yuan considered strong government perfectly compatible with a dynamic private economy. Indeed, he saw merchants' quest for private profit as an essential ingredient of public policy. Official economic domains (the salt gabelle, the transport of grain) might be run by private merchants more effectively and with ultimate benefit to the state. Sea transport of grain to Beijing, Wei believed, rather than shipment through the Grand Canal, would take advantage of the unprecedented growth of coastal commerce since the late seventeenth century and would thereby transmute merchant enterprise into public benefit. Capital for mining enterprises could be raised more effectively from private merchants than from government treasuries. Along with many of his contemporaries, Wei recognized the indefeasible claims of the market upon social behavior. It seemed futile, for instance, for the government to issue paper currency, because even imperial decrees could not force the people to accept it.[37]

Nevertheless, Wei Yuan was notably unsqueamish about coercion: in the hands of the ruler, power existed in order to be used: "To wield a sword but not cut; to grasp an oar but not cross [the river]: nobody is that foolish."[38] As he contemplated the accelerating disaster of his age, Wei Yuan placed his hopes on two visions, which seemed to him quite compatible: a greater scope for political involvement by the established elite; and an authoritarianism that would not shrink from the conduct of the Hegemons—power-

---

[37]Lin Manhong (Lin Man-houng), "Two Social Theories Revealed: Statecraft Controversies Over China's Monetary Crisis, 1808–1854," *Late Imperial China* 12.2 (Dec. 1991), pp. 14–15; WYJ, p. 423.

[38]WYJ, p. 38.

holders so despised by moralistic Confucian historians, but so good at keeping order.

Shortly after Wei's death in 1857 there emerged some of the characteristic themes that we associate with modern Chinese politics. One was the "principled criticism" (*qing-yi*) movement, in which high-ranking officials became targets of political attack for having appeased foreign aggressors. This agitation of "outs" against "ins" had begun in the aftermath of the Opium War, but emerged as a major political force only as it became associated with modern nationalism. Another was the effort to graft Western industrial technology onto a Confucian cultural base. Such an effort explicitly proclaimed the cultural neutrality of modern technology. If True King and Hegemon could be distinguished only by their intentions, and not by their actions; if a scholar could throw himself into the practical details of government without imperiling his moral character—then ethics and culture were effectively insulated from the technical details of government. From the ethical neutrality of political technique to the cultural neutrality of machine technology is but a short mental step. Champions of "self-strengthening" (many of them admirers of Wei Yuan) believed that the "substance" (*ti*) of Confucian culture was essentially invulnerable to the "utility" (*yong*) of Western technology. Although Wei Yuan did not live to see "self-strengthening," we may suppose that such an assumption would have caused him little anxiety.

That broader political participation should have been associated so readily with the enhancement of state power, rather than with its limitation, suggests to us the distinctive, native origins of the modern Chinese state. Wealth and power for the state, broader political commitment and participation for the literati: both (and the connection between them) were already on China's constitutional agenda in late imperial times. Though neither vision had been inspired by the West, Chinese were soon to begin importing Western (and Japanese) methods to achieve them. In the next chapter, we shall consider how far such Western methods affected another influential nineteenth-century thinker, Feng Guifen; and how they clashed with some of China's more authoritarian traditions.

CHAPTER 2

Reform on Trial

Before Wei Yuan had been five years in his grave, China had become a client state of the Western powers. Only by accepting the foreigners' demands for commercial, diplomatic, and missionary privilege could the court obtain the respite—and the Western arms—to defeat the great rebellions that now ravaged China's heartland. The year 1860, when the court accepted the foreigners' terms, was a turning point in China's constitutional development.

Foreigners [handwritten margin note]

To appreciate the importance of the 1860s settlement (the Peking Convention, following the entry of the Anglo-French forces into the capital and the ratification of the Treaty of Tientsin of 1858), we must consider that China's constitutional agenda was cumulative. Old problems remained unsolved even as new ones were added. And it was quickly understood by a few men that even as the rebellions were being suppressed with Western military technology, old constitutional problems might perhaps be addressed with Western political technology. Among the literati of the lower Yangzi provinces who took refuge in the treaty port of Shanghai in the spring of 1860 was an old friend of Wei Yuan: Feng Guifen had fled his native Suzhou in May 1860, as the Taiping rebel army attacked. Less than a year's sojourn in Shanghai, now the main beachhead of Western power and influence, was enough to acquaint him with some Western political notions that seemed relevant to his longstanding concerns about China's domestic problems.

Feng Guifen (1809–74), like Wei Yuan, has been admired by Western historians, and for similar ethnocentric reasons. Feng is praised as a pioneer of the self-strengthening (*ziqiang*) movement, the official effort to graft Western technology onto a Chinese cultural base. But his significance for China's constitutional history, I would suggest, lies in his effort to transform an older Chinese agenda.

Feng's outlook can be distinguished from Wei Yuan's not only by his willingness to give concrete form to what Wei discussed only in theoretical terms, but also by his adaptation of Western political ideas to the issues of the old agenda. Although Western historians have emphasized his admiration for Western machine technology, a careful examination of his Shanghai writings suggests that he was even more attracted to Western political technology. Considering his background, this can only be explained by his thorough immersion in China's internal problems.

Precocious and brilliant even by Suzhou standards, Feng had won a doctorate at age thirty-two and had been appointed a Hanlin academician in Beijing. As happened with his friend Wei Yuan, his years in the capital raised him

56 Reform on Trial

above his provincial origins and linked him with a national network of colleagues. (It makes no more sense to classify Feng as a Suzhou landlord than to classify Mao Zedong as a Hunanese farmer).[1] Like Wei, he considered himself part of a national, not a provincial, elite; and the essence of his constitutional thinking was to place his provincial concerns in a national framework. These two men, with their official patrons, participated in a reformist coterie that was bound together by two interlocking sets of concerns. In the foreground was the foreign threat. In the background, and seemingly the more intractable problem, was the economic disaster in the Yangzi provinces.

The massive commercial and demographic growth of the eighteenth century had inflamed economic competition in all spheres of life, not least in government. The commercialization of government occurred as middleman-entrepreneurs attached themselves to the tax system (see Chapter 3). Unchecked tax-farming impoverished taxpayers at the same time as it diverted revenue from the state. Among the worst offenders were functionaries of the centrally managed Grain Transport Administration, which was in effect a free-wheeling taxation agency that preyed upon officialdom and populace alike. A series of small-scale local rebellions had already been incited by it during the 1840s, and the elites of the most heavily taxed provinces (including Feng Guifen's notoriously overtaxed home region of Suzhou) had reason to believe that worse was in store.

Although local officials were themselves victims of this system, it was the officials who were the targets of farmers'

[1]Cf. James Polachek, "Gentry Hegemony: Suzhou in the T'ung-chih Restoration," in Frederic Wakeman and Carolyn Grant, eds., Conflict and Control in Late Imperial China (Berkeley: University of California Press, 1975), pp. 211–56.

anger. Back in his home county during 1849, Feng observed the smoldering fuse in local society: "The commoners have accumulated such resentment toward the magistrates that it has entered their bones and marrow. If an incident should arise [to provoke them], people's minds will turn toward violence."[2] Indeed, within a few years the Taiping rebels would be recruiting mass armies from among the disaffected Yangzi farmers.

For both Wei Yuan and Feng Guifen, broader literati participation was to be the source of the heightened national energy needed to resist the West. They may also have seen it as a fulcrum for dislodging the entrenched interests behind the Grain Transport Administration. We have seen how Wei Yuan was preoccupied with mobilizing such broad support and furnishing it with an acceptable rationale. But Wei treated such constitutional questions in very general terms. In the face of the unparalleled disasters that struck China in the years following Wei's death in 1857, Feng Guifen, fifteen years his junior, was driven to give them more concrete form.

Feng's forty *Essays of Protest* (*Jiaobinlu kangyi*), composed apparently during his first year of Shanghai exile, contained two types of proposal.[3] The first concerned major

---

[2]Feng Guifen, *Xianzhitang ji* 5:21 (letter of 1849).

[3]The title means literally, "Essays of protest from the cottage where one studies the ancient system of the Zhou" (*bin* refers to the original homeland of the Zhou conquerors). The edition cited here is the convenient one of 1897 (reprint: Taipei, Xuehai chubanshe, 1967). Feng's own preface is dated November 1861. The exact number of essays written during that year is uncertain. Zeng Guofan, to whom Feng sent a manuscript copy in 1862, mentions in his diary the numbers "forty-two" and "forty" (entries for 8 Nov. 1862 and 14 Dec. 1864). Feng himself may have culled certain essays when he sent them around. He omitted the more radical proposals (including the two considered here) from his collected works, the corpus by which he preferred to be evaluated by later generations. An edition edited in 1884 by

technical improvements in government operations, whether engineering (changing the course of the Yellow River) or fiscal (defanging the Grain Transport Administration and reforming the traditional salt gabelle). The second consisted of constitutional changes that would reallocate political power and status, both within the bureaucracy and outside it. The technical proposals resembled the agenda of the reformists of the 1820s to 1830s, the period when Lin Zexu and Wei Yuan were active in provincial administration. The constitutional proposals were more radical, and there are unmistakable signs that they were influenced by Western ideas.[4]

Thanks to a recent archival discovery, our approach to Feng's writings will take a somewhat unusual direction. A quarter-century after Feng's death, during the great Reform Movement of 1898, the ardent young reformist emperor Guangxu (who had admired Feng's essays for some years) circulated the *Essays of Protest* to government officials in Beijing and demanded comments. The original responses, preserved in the imperial archives, give us a re-

---

Feng's sons contains forty essays, which was probably the original number. The 1897 edition contains ten more essays, of which eight are from Feng's collected works, *Xianzhitang ji*, Jiaobinlu edition, 1876; reprint: Taipei, Wenhai chubanshe, 1981. I am indebted to Kwang-ching Liu for guidance on this point.

[4]Feng's debt to Western ideas was perceived by his contemporaries. For example, Zhao Liewen, a member of Zeng Guofan's staff who read Feng's essays in the spring of 1863, pronounced the proposal to elect high functionaries to be "a practice of the barbarians" (*i-fa*). However, the essay on rural functionaries struck Zhao as merely "extending Gu Yanwu's ideas," as Feng indeed had acknowledged. See *Nengjingzhai riji* (Taibei: Xuesheng shuju, 1964), 1119–20. An authoritative 1993 article from Beijing emphasizes that Feng's interest in the West went well beyond mere technical subjects. The author forbears to mention, however, Feng's proposal on the election of high officials. Ding Weizhi, "Jiaobinlu kangyi yu Zhongguo wenhua jindaihua," *Lishi yanjiu* (1993.5), pp. 74–91.

vealing view of how Feng's views were perceived by some
rather conventional political minds.[5]

Indeed, it is precisely the conventional character of the
responses that is so valuable as we attempt to understand
the difficulty of establishing a constitutional monarchy in
the late Qing era. The evolution of China's modern state
suggests that (as the late Chairman Mao would ruefully
admit if he could be asked) it is the conventional percep-
tions, rather than the radical ones, that have dominated
China's modern history. In these comments on what is,
even for today's China, a set of radical proposals, we are
witnessing the impact of unusual ideas on the generality of
late-imperial officialdom. Though the reception of these
ideas was not uniformly hostile, we shall observe certain
reactions of extreme sensitivity where constitutional principles were called into question. The alarm generated by
Feng's proposals, I believe, was not just a momentary set-
back in some inevitable process of constitutional change,
but rather a confirmation of certain fundamental and du-
rable values of Chinese public life.

Here I shall sample the debate by exploring the reactions to two essays—one relating to national institutions
and the other to local ones—that embody the core of
Feng's constitutional thought. One advocates broadening

[5]These documents were first described by Li Kan and Gong Shuduo in "Wuxu
bianfa shiqi dui *Jiaobinlu kangyi* di yici pinglun: jieshao gugong bowuyuan Ming-
Qing dang'anbu suocang *Jiaobinlu kangyi* qianzhuben," *Wenwu* (1978.7), pp. 53–59. I
have had access only to unnumbered manuscript transcriptions of these documents
and can refer to them only as *qianzhu* (comments), with the author of the comment
indicated in each case. They are intended for eventual publication by the First Historical Archives, Beijing. On Feng Guifen's political thought, see Lu Shiqiang (Lü
Shih-ch'iang), "Feng Guifen de zhengzhi sixiang," *Zhonghua wenhua fuxing yuekan*
4.2 (1971), pp. 5–12.

political participation by subjecting high officials to election by lower-ranking officials. Another proposes a denser infrastructure of political control in rural villages. Both broader participation and denser political control are salient elements of China's modern political history; yet in Feng's case, they seemed to be rooted in old constitutional concerns.

"Making the evaluation of officials a public process" (*gong chuzhi yi*) is placed first among the forty essays, and its sweeping implications suggest that Feng saw it as a precondition for all that followed.[6] Existing practice was to qualify officials through written examinations, and to choose among those qualified by relying on the judgment of a small body of high officials. "How can this do other than render 'talent and virtue' mere empty, baseless criteria?" Feng demanded. Surely the views of "myriad men" were a more reliable gauge of a candidate's worth. Feng now proposed to make many high posts subject to nomination by the bureaucracy at large. Even low-ranking officials would be required to submit annual nominations for ministerial posts. "The Board of Civil Appointment would record [the nominations] and rank the nominees according to the number of nominations they received. When a vacancy comes open, the men listed would be appointed in order [of their position on the list]. Anyone not nominated could not be ranked." The power to nominate local officials would be even more broadly dispersed, to include even first-degree holders and village elders.

The effect would be to reduce the power of high officials to install their personal followers in office, and thus to

public office

[6]"Gong chuzhi yi" in Feng, *Jiaobinlu kangyi*, pp. 1–2b.

make the highest central officials responsible, in some degree, to the bureaucracy at large; and local officials to the
elites of their communities. Yet Feng makes no explicit
case for the principle of representation, or for the limitation of power.

reduce power of high officials

Feng acknowledges no foreign source for this proposal,
and indeed cites a number of Chinese authorities that, he
insists, fit the spirit of it. Yet one telltale track gives him
away: his assertion that, in weighing opinions, the thing to
do is to *count them*. No idea is less congenial to the Chinese governmental system than that of equally weighted
votes, for the simple reason that one man's opinion is assuredly not equivalent to the opinion of any other; men
are, after all, differentiated by both virtue and education.
Yet, in our exploration of Wei Yuan's thought, we have already observed the conundrum underlying Chinese social
structure: though political power and status were une-
qually distributed, the literati shared a certain equality of
cultural status. In their effort to broaden political participation, both Wei Yuan and Feng Guifen emphasized the
shared-status aspect of literati identity. The idea that all
literati shared a common and legitimate concern for public
affairs was, it seems to me, a *transitional concept* of some
importance in early modern politics. Before long, nationalism would add another component of shared status:
common membership (that is, citizenship) in a society that
was coterminous with a national polity (that is, a nation-
state). The latter was a more volatile idea, one that extended indefinitely into the commoner population; and
one that, by the late nineteenth century, was inflamed by a
fear of racial extinction.

no foreign source

Although reactions to this proposal in 1898 were almost

uniformly hostile, the grounds for objection were not trivial: they were phrased as a concern for public good over private advantage, and for principle over opportunism. Transferring such powers to lower levels of the elite would allow private interests to invade what should be an objective appointment procedure. If the state were to rely on the opinions of local elite about whether an official should be promoted, those low-status elites "would not give due attention to [the official's] feelings and prestige" (*wulun zhan'gu qingmian*) and would use the occasion to manipulate him (*xiezhi*).[7] But high officials are expected to be impartial in assessing merit among their subordinates. If they "hew firmly to the public interest, then there will be no difficulty getting good men."[8]

The pursuit of private ends would lead inevitably to the formation of factions, wrote Feng's critics. As soon as factions formed to "promote the interests of their members," the chances of getting good men into office would be remote. Indeed, once the appointment power falls into the hands of factions, "nothing will be heard of the upright and decent" (who by their nature would shun factions).[9] Only a small, high-placed group of officials could attain an objective view; bringing in the mass of educated men would make such objectivity impossible. Inevitably, "crafty officials" will all "flip the dust off their caps [preparatory to assuming their new posts] and congratulate one another," and the sincere, unassuming aspirant, whatever his merit, will have no chance at all.[10]

[7]*Qianzhu*, comment of Lai Qingjian.
[8]*Qianzhu*, comment of Yanqing.
[9]*Qianzhu*, comment of Wang Zhensheng.
[10]*Qianzhu*, comment of Puqiu.

The proposal was harshly criticized by Feng's old patron, Li Hongzhang, who had known Feng well during his Shanghai sojourn. If the power to recommend officials were extended to lower ranks, then "everyone would have his private interest to promote," and the truth would never emerge. Because high officials already were responsible for evaluating their subordinates, they should retain the corresponding power to recommend them or impeach them. The impartiality of high officials, wrote Li, must not be swayed by pressures from below. Feng's proposal, he declared,

> was modeled on the system by which the American Congress selects officials, without understanding its evils. [In that system,] those below seek their private advantage, those above protect their clients. At its worst, the system amounts to seeking office through bribery. Perceptive people in that country are already well aware of this.[11]

What the critics feared was not some abstract diminution of the traditional appointive power, but a political system dominated by factional strife, a scramble for advantage, and the exaltation of purely private ends. In such a system, they insisted, not the cream but the scum would rise to the surface. We must regard this fear as the deeply ingrained attitude of a tiny, privileged elite, which understood its monopoly of political power through the mandarin premise that education raised men above petty, private considerations; and that high officials, specially qualified by education, must therefore embody a purer view of the public interest than those below them. The inevitable exceptions were to be dealt with by the existing system, in

[11]*Qianzhu*, comment of Li Hongzhang.

which all superior officials were in theory held personally accountable for the behavior of men whom they recommended, as well as for impeaching subordinates guilty of impropriety or ineptitude. At the apex of the system, anchoring it in the purest public-mindedness, was the monarch, who presumably owed favors to no man. That partiality and factions flourished in actual practice, did not make them acceptable in theory.

In his proposal on official appointments, Feng was advocating an expanded political role for the lower bureaucracy and local literati. In the second essay I shall treat here, Feng deals with the dangerous volatility of local society by aiming directly at the problem of predatory middlemen: the hustlers who had inserted themselves into local government as a way of making money. His essay "On Restoring the System of Local Headmen" (*Fu xiangzhi yi*) was inspired by a familiar example from late antiquity: the rural government system of the Qin and Han periods, in which "district" and "neighborhood" officers formed a fine network of control in the villages, a system admired by Feng's seventeenth-century mentor Gu Yanwu.

Over the centuries of Chinese imperial history, no constitutional issue generated more heat than the proper character of rural government: how were the interests of the state and the local communities to be balanced? Were natural, communitarian organizations (the lineage, the local cult, the village elders) the best instruments for ordering society and nourishing the state? Would it be necessary to use a government-supervised system of mutual responsibility, or a more ramified bureaucracy? How could the power of local elites be socialized to accord with the purposes of the state? Such questions gained urgency from the population pressure, the economic insecurity, and the smoldering popular temper of the nineteenth century.

Feng's proposal for rural government must be viewed in the light of his overriding concern to rationalize the rural tax system and so forestall rebellion. Reducing special privilege and breaking the power of the Grain Transport Administration were vital first steps. But even tax reform would not solve the problem of bringing officials and commoners into harmony. The rebellious temper of the countryside required a mechanism to build trust, mediate legal cases, and defuse crises. Feng's solution was a new kind of middleman, who would be chosen by the villagers themselves through paper ballots.

Like Wei Yuan, Feng had been inspired by the writings of the seventeenth-century scholar Gu Yanwu. Gu's famous dictum, "When high officials are numerous, the age will be in decline; when lesser officials are numerous, the age will flourish," was considered admirable but visionary (how could all those lower officials be fed and supervised?).[12] Yet Feng believed that the pressures of China's overcrowded village society required something better than the informal delegation of power to local bosses. Surely the solution was not to expand the numbers of subcounty "assistants" (*liyuan*), whose social origins Feng considered "motley" and whose aspirations were "undistinguished." Such men, often from distant places, obtained their rank by purchase and depended wholly on what money they could scrape from their jobs. They "act like dogs and horses to the rich and treat the poor as fish and meat." In-

---

[12]Quoted by Feng, in "Fu xiangzhi yi" (*Jiaobinlu kangyi*, p. 10); the original source is Gu's "Xiangting zhi zhi," *Yuanchaoben rizhilu* (Taipei: Minglun chuban-she, 1970), p. 231.

deed it was such as these, along with the notorious clerks, who had so disastrously commercialized local government.

The solution Feng proposed was to use local men whom the populace would trust because they had chosen them. They would have quasi-official status but would be chosen by groups of 100 and 1,000 households. Nominees would be drawn from the level beneath the much-mistrusted licentiates (*shengyuan*). Here again was the unmistakable imprint of the West: each villager was to write his name and his nominee on a slip of paper; the slips would be counted, and the man with the most slips would be appointed.

The 1898 reactions to this proposal revolved around two main points: (1) the necessity for a rigid line of demarcation between officials and nonofficials; (2) fear that a quasi-official elite would arrogate power to themselves and disregard the public interest.

How would it serve the public interest to establish, in addition to regular bureaucrats, "numerous men who act as officials without actually being officials"?[13] An intermediate stratum that was neither official nor commoner was inconsistent with the realities of rural society: "The people's disposition (*minfeng*) is not that of antiquity. If the local functionaries have no authority, then the people will not obey them. If they do have authority, then they are bound to be authoritarian in their methods, and the people will still not obey them."[14]

Such an intermediate stratum would not only be useless: it might also be dangerous. The experiences of the

[13]*Qianzhu*, comment of Wenzheng.
[14]*Qianzhu*, comment of Wang Zhensheng.

mid-century rebellions had reinforced official fears of local leaders with too much power. With the slightest encouragement, "bad gentry and evil managers" (*diaojin liedong*)[15] would arrogate power to themselves and exert improper pressure on local bureaucrats. Here again is the fear of manipulation from below (*xiezhi* or *qianzhi*), by which local interests would nullify the authority of the magistrate.[16] So deep was the official mistrust of nonofficial middlemen that those proposed by Feng could not be distinguished, by his critics, from the predatory local strongmen who, since the suppression of the Taipings, controlled much of village China.[17] What could be a greater threat to law and order? To make matters worse, asserted the critics, Feng's new stratum of middlemen would not even function as advertised. Instead of passing information upward through the system, they would tend to conceal it, thus rendering the whole system pointless. The magistrate himself was supposed to remain close to the people. Why impede his work with a new layer of intermediaries?[18]

Finally, the 1898 reactions to Feng's *Essays of Protest* are epitomized by one of his severest critics, the Hanlin academician Chen Ding.[19] The comments of this eccentric and

[15]The term *jin* refers to holders of academic degrees, and *dong* to local notables appointed by magistrates to fill local administrative jobs. The *dong* could be in charge of their community in general, or of a specific task such as supervising militia or managing waterworks. Though *dong* were often degree holders, their degrees mattered less than their local influence.

[16]*Qianzhu*, comments of Yang Shixie, Puqiu, and Zhao Erchen.

[17]*Qianzhu*, comment of Zhao Erchen.

[18]*Qianzhu*, comment of Puqiu.

[19]Chen, a Hunanese scholar, had been appointed to the Hanlin Academy in 1880 and later was promoted to Junior Compiler, a rank that entitled him to remain at the Academy. For information on Chen, I am indebted to an unpublished manuscript by Kong Xiangji, cited here by permission of the author.

evidently fearless scholar illustrate how imperfectly the term "conservative" describes the opponents of reform. Chen was hardly a stereotypical foe of Western culture. In his comments to Feng's essay "On Proper Management of the Barbarians," Chen advocated that Chinese master foreign languages extensively; and even offered such outrageous ideas as intermarriage with foreigners (beginning with "high officials," the purpose being to gather intelligence!), and cooptation of Christianity as one of China's officially venerated cults, along with Buddhism.[20] The effects of these inflammatory proposals on conventional minds, on the eve of the Boxer uprising, can well be imagined.

Yet to Feng's constitutional proposals, Chen's reactions were scathingly orthodox. To draw appointment nominations from lower bureaucrats would lead to corruption and fragmentation of the state. What appeared to be a "public" process would merely provide a feast for private interests. "Actually," he wrote, "the opinion of the crowd cannot be formed by public interest, and so-called 'public' opinion must really be motivated by private interests." And how could one hope for impartial evaluations of merit in such quarters? "If we transfer the power of appointment downward into the hands of lower officials, seeking evaluations through all sorts of perverse utterances," total chaos would result. In place of impartial administration would emerge rule by powerful factions.

It is not hard for officials to avoid offending the powerful. And whomever the powerful favor, the whole realm favors. [In an-

[20]For a transcription of parts of Chen Ding's *Jiaobinlu kangyi bielun,* an unpublished manuscript in the First Historical Archives, and for biographical information on Chen, I am indebted to Kong Xiangji. All my citations of Chen refer to this transcription.

cient times the philosopher] Mencius spoke thus, and how much the more must it be so with today's officials. Through collusion [with the powerful] they can gain reputations as "meritorious officials"; and what is called "public selection" will actually be [the machinations of] one man.

Under such a regime, office-seekers would collude with one another to curry favor and appease the powerful. "If this is the way they gain their reputations, what time will they have to spare for the interests of the State?"

From this acerbic critic, Feng's proposals for reinstituting "local headmen" fared no better. The prospect is one of naked greed and rampant intimidation.

Power attracts any man, all the more if there is a salary attached, and if he can manage affairs and assume the dignity of an official . . . At nomination time, not only will groups scurry about touting their own merits; lineages and kin-groups will follow, all brandishing their standards. Or worse, there will be men who rely on powerful gentry to promote their factions and to force the villagers to elect them.

And Chen's critique reflects the conventional scorn of lower-level middlemen:

Upright scholars and decent men all have their own families to manage. Rich households have their livelihoods. Such persons would never be willing to assume this kind of [low-level administrative] post. Those who would want to are only the evil licentiates and disreputable *jiansheng* (*diaosheng liejian*) and vagrants with no means of support.[21]

---

[21]*Jiansheng* were nominally "students of the imperial academy," a purchased status with no academic standing. They were, however, eligible to sit for the provincial-level examination at Shuntian (Beijing), which many actually did. Among county magistrates, however, *jiansheng* were scorned as *arrivistes* and troublemakers.

Indeed, Feng's proposals were unmistakably the first steps toward Western-style democracy. But look at the dire results in the West!

In Western countries there are different religions and parties that frequently fight one another. When they kill kings and fathers, they do not regard it as perverse. When they oppress the people, they do not regard it as blameworthy. Is this not the result of the people's having seized power?

May we not, finally, look beyond the usual "conservative" or "reactionary" labels in our efforts to understand Feng's critics, and through them the backlash against the 1898 reformers? We are verging here, I would suggest, upon the inner core of Chinese authoritarianism, a system of beliefs about human behavior that did not necessarily dissolve with the emergence of the modern state.

Why did public authorities exist? Surely to keep private interests in check. The belief was founded on a conviction that public values were not adequately internalized to permit people to pursue their private interests unchecked. It follows that political competition and the resulting factional struggle can only result in damage to the public interest. Only the regular bureaucracy can prevent the elite as a whole from exercising illegitimate power in pursuit of private interests. Only the upper layers of the ruling group can attain the kind of objectivity needed to keep the bureaucracy as a whole from pursuing private or factional ends. And at the very top, only the emperor can ensure that the system as a whole is directed toward the public interest. These assumptions in turn assume that the higher the official rank, the more objective the view of the public interest.

The critics' social vision was a bleak one. It was summed

up in the conventional lament, "The disposition of the people [or of the age] is not that of antiquity." By this was meant that present-day China was a long way from the classical vision of ancient society as a utopia in which every man had a natural concern for the public interest, a golden age when public values were so internalized that authoritarian coercion was unnecessary.

In the present age, however, authority was needed to keep private interests in check. Assuming that top officials would do so presents a vexing problem: how could you be sure that top officials were not themselves acting on behalf of private interests? The problem ceased to exist if you believed that higher officials would inevitably have a more objective view of the public interest than lower ones, and that officialdom as a whole would have a more objective view than mere private persons. This view was reinforced by the moralistic assumptions about factional activity. It was believed that only base motives could lead men to join factions. Factional self-promotion is identified with a certain character type (the "crafty official," *qiaohuan*). A man who was decent, sincere, self-respecting, would not compete that way. The business of "getting ahead," through patronage and favoritism, though universally practiced, was never publicly approved. So factions were not bad merely because they divided the polity, but because those who joined them were likely to be scoundrels. By a charming illogic, because high officials were likely to be worthy men, they could not have attained their positions by behaving like scoundrels!

Though lower bureaucrats were supposed to be controlled by their superiors, the greatest threat to the public interest was seen to lie outside the bureaucracy: in the multiple strata of middlemen who competed for public resources. These middlemen always threatened to arrogate to themselves, for private gain, powers that properly belonged to the bureaucracy. Giving authority to a new stratum of quasi-bureaucrats in local society, as Feng proposed, was just asking for trouble. Such men would inevitably wield *illegitimate power* (I think that is how we must understand the terms *xiezhi* and *bachi*) at the expense of the public interest. The lowly first-degree holders (*shengyuan*), who were not fully subject to bureaucratic discipline, were particularly suspect. So reasoned Chen Ding.

Feng himself would have understood this line of reasoning. He was well aware of the danger of unchecked local power. His program for rebuilding local society was a step away from the unregulated rule of local militia-leaders and "gentry managers" (officially sanctioned local bosses). With firm ties to the upper bureaucracy, Feng was no liberal; nor do his writings reveal any intimations whatever of popular sovereignty or popular rights. His position was, however, close to that of his intellectual forerunner, Wei Yuan: he believed that the public interest was more widely internalized, among the elite, than conventional wisdom assumed. The lower-ranking elite could be trusted to pursue the public interest if they were accorded a carefully measured degree of political participation. This was entirely in line with Wei Yuan's effort to inspire the broader elite with greater interest in public affairs.

But only a tendentious modern historiography can deny Feng's critics their principles. Consider the situation as they must have seen it. The mid-century rebellions had been suppressed, but at a terrible cost. The government's authority had been dangerously diluted. At the top was an uneasy alliance between the court and powerful provincial leaders. Control over the land-tax had, to some extent, been lost to private middlemen. Within the elite itself, the power of private wealth (through the purchase of ranks and offices) had increased dangerously. Privatization of public resources was rampant on every level of government. In these circumstances, to reestablish the authority of the regular bureaucracy was the way to keep Chinese society from total breakdown. Indeed, proposals to devolve power upon wider segments of society must have seemed invitations to chaos and corruption everywhere. The principled response was to seek greater objectivity and more general enforcement of the public interest over private interests. If the public interest did not rule every man's mind, what but bureaucratic control could hold anarchy at bay?

〜

The idea that there exists a "public interest," as distinct from the sum of private interests, seems an anachronism in the modern world. The liberal democracies have largely lost the capacity even to express such a view. Bizarre as the conception of "public interest" may seem in contemporary America, that conception was a dominant theme in the early republic. Although there was lively disagreement as to how such a "public interest" or "public good" might be realized in the practice of government, its existence was not seriously doubted.

The great vehicle for popularizing the principles of the proposed new Constitution of 1787, *The Federalist*, provides abundant examples of this faith.[22] For our present

_____

[22]Eighty-five papers, signed "Publius," arguing the case for ratification of the

purposes, the essential question addressed by the essays that make up *The Federalist* is how to reconcile the public interest with a multiplicity of private interests. Private interests, expressed through "factions," would always exist among the populace. In the celebrated tenth essay, James Madison wrote that one of the advantages of "a well-constructed Union" was that it tended "to break and control the violence of faction."[23] Popular government had widely been criticized because "the public good is disregarded in the conflicts of rival parties," so that "an interested and overbearing majority" would promote its aims in defiance of the public and of legitimate minority interests. Madison elaborated: "By a faction, I understand a number of citizens, whether amounting to a majority or minority of the whole, who are united and actuated by some common impulse of passion, or of interest, adverse to the rights of other citizens, or to the permanent and aggregate interests of the community." "Factions," however, Madison believed to be a constant presence in society. Though they are by nature "adverse" to the public interest, their causes are "sown in the nature of man." Government could not protect the public interest by stamping them out, which would erase liberty itself. Nor could the public interest be made universal by changing (or as the Chinese would say, "transforming"—*hua*) the character of the citi-

---

Federal Constitution by the states, appeared serially in the New York press between October 1787 and May 1788. The first edition of *The Federalist*, which brought the papers together in two volumes with an introduction by Alexander Hamilton, appeared in 1788. Fifty of the papers are attributed to Hamilton, thirty to James Madison, and five to John Jay.

[23]Madison's tenth essay is referred to here as it appears in *The Federalist, or The New Constitution: Papers by Alexander Hamilton, James Madison and John Jay* (New York: Modern Library, 1941), pp. 53–62.

zenry, "by giving to every citizen the same opinions, the same passions, and the same interests," which was impossible, given the "diversity in the faculties of men."

Despite Madison's pessimistic view of faction as an irrepressible outgrowth of human nature, his remedy was astonishingly sanguine. Citizens might have their private interests, but they had also an innate civic consciousness. However vulnerable to the forces of passion and private interest, ordinary men had the civic sense to recognize "men of virtue and wisdom" as their proper representatives.[24] In a republic big enough, the passions of faction would be filtered through these "men of virtue and wisdom," whose elevated view of the public interest would save society from faction's destructive effects.

Madison's resort to men who, by their "virtue and wisdom," are better suited than their compatriots to discern the public interest has led critics to label him an elitist; and the connection of "virtue and wisdom" to high public office would not have seemed unreasonable to an imperial mandarin. If Madison was not offering a "Chinese" solution of "enlightened statesmen," he was also not abandoning the idea that some men are more likely than others to discern the public interest. By virtue of their position, the people's representatives "may best discern the true interest of their country," and their "patriotism and love of justice will be least likely to sacrifice it to temporary or partial considerations."[25]

[24]*The Papers of James Madison*, ed. William Hutchison et al. (Chicago: University of Chicago Press, 1962), vol. II, p. 163; quoted in Michael T. Gibbons, "The Public Sphere, Commercial Society, and The Federalist Papers," in *The Federalists, the Antifederalists, and the American Political Tradition* (Wilson Carey McWilliams and Michael T. Gibbons, eds., Westport, Conn: Greenwood Press, 1992), pp. 119–20.

[25]*The Federalist*, p. 60. For a general discussion of how the concept of public in-

Yet Madison's sense of the public interest was in one crucial respect quite distinct from the mandarin one. The representative principle rested on the premise that civic virtue, though specially concentrated in men of virtue and wisdom, was in fact widespread among the populace, even though in a form less refined. Republicanism depended on it: without "virtue in the people," good government is inconceivable.[26] So the disposition of the people was, in its civic sense, equal (as the Chinese would say) to "that of antiquity." This essential quality, which made representative government possible, also precluded a fundamental distinction between rulers and ruled.

By contrast, the pessimism of Feng's mandarin critics precludes even the possibility of effective representation. If ordinary men lacked civic sense, they might rightly be feared by guardians of the public interest. If even officials were so vulnerable to the blandishments of faction leaders that they could not be trusted to express opinions on the leadership, how much less trustworthy the commoners? Without civic virtue, villagers and bureaucrats alike would easily be deceived by the wiles of ambitious villains. With civic virtue so unevenly distributed, a government of superior men is needed to "transform" the mass of the people. Madison, by contrast, considers "the present genius of the people of America" as quite incapable of electing a body of representatives "who would be disposed to form and pursue a scheme of tyranny or treachery."[27]

---

terest fared historically, and its treatment by social scientists, see J. A. W. Gunn, "Public Interest," in Terence Ball et al., eds., *Political Innovation and Conceptual Change* (Cambridge, Eng.: Cambridge University Press, 1989), pp. 194–210.

[26]Madison, *Papers*, vol. 11, p. 163, quoted in Gibbons, "Public Sphere," p. 119.

[27]*The Federalist* No. 55, p. 363.

Was civic virtue in fact so rare among ordinary Chinese? Not at all: in every corner of the empire, community service was not only thriving, but even served as a mark of legitimate elite status. Local gazetteers contain abundant evidence, not only of local pride, but also of concrete sacrifice for community well-being in the form of charity. A wealthy merchant could signify his membership in the local elite, not only by buying ranks and titles, but by performing such "good works" (*shanxing*) as would earn him a biographical notice in the county gazetteer, and a place on the engraved stele of the local temple association.

Nor was natural civic virtue neglected by Chinese political writers. Although the blissful unselfishness of "antiquity" remained a remote vision, the natural affection of men for their home communities might yet prove the firmest surety for good government. The most celebrated expression of this view, and that most often cited in the last decades of the empire, was "On the System of Bureaucratic Government" (*Junxian lun*), by the seventeenth-century writer Gu Yanwu. (We shall have occasion to assess this tradition, and its effects on late-imperial politics, in the fourth chapter.)

But if there was acknowledged to be some degree of immanent civic virtue among ordinary Chinese, it was believed to work best in a local setting. To conceive of it on the national scale—the arena of greatest concern to Feng Guifen's critics—proved exceedingly difficult. It was as if the home-town civism that might work for good government in a county would become deformed and ultimately destroyed in a national setting.[28]

[28]One is reminded here of Montesquieu's assumption that republican virtue, as a concern for public over private interests, could exist only in a small political framework. Opponents of Madison and his *Federalist* colleagues drew upon Mon-

May we, then, concede to Feng's critics a degree of seriousness about the future of their world, given what they considered the precariousness of the public interest in the conditions of their time? Lacking representative government, which few Chinese of the time could even conceive of, what was to ensure that the public interest was protected? One reasonable solution (indeed the one that most twentieth-century Chinese governments have adopted) was to strengthen bureaucratic control, and thereby to ensure the kind of higher objectivity that could rise above narrow, private interests. Lacking alternatives, authoritarian leadership by regular bureaucrats seemed entirely reasonable to these men.

This approach can be distinguished from those which hold (1) that social norms are so internalized that everyone, on whatever level, will have the public interest in mind, and hence authoritarian leadership is not needed; or (2) that private selfish interests, when aggregated, will tend to produce a public interest (the "invisible hand"); or (3) that the majority power should prevail, whatever its effect on the rest of society, and that no abstract "public interest" exists. In the liberal democracies, these three views coexist in uneasy balance.

Feng Guifen's critics believed the first to be a beautiful but vain illusion: "The people's disposition is not that of

---

tesquieu's warning that "In an extensive republic the public good is sacrificed to a thousand private views." Quoted in Paul Peterson, "Antifederalist Thought in Contemporary American Politics." In Josephine F. Pacheco, ed., *Antifederalism: The Legacy of George Mason* (Fairfax, Va: George Mason University Press, 1992), p. 130; also see Abraham Kupersmith, "Montesquieu and the Ideological Strain in Antifederalist Thought," in McWilliams and Gibbons, eds., *The Federalists, the Antifederalists, and the American Political Tradition*, pp. 47–75.

antiquity." They regarded the second as an absurd fallacy, and presumably would have regarded the third—if they could have imagined it at all—as a vision of hell. A society ruled by selfish interests, in which opportunism always conquers principle, in which power and money crush all other human concerns, in which the political process raises incompetent or evil men to positions of leadership: who would want to live there?

CHAPTER 3

Maoist Agriculture and the Old Regime

The Leiyang Revolt and Its Fiscal Background

Even as British gunfire resounded on the Chinese coast in the early 1840s, a gathering storm of rebellion flashed ominously along the dark horizon of the interior provinces.

The soil in the mountainous county of Leiyang, in southern Hunan, was so poor that "a good farmer may toil all his life yet never reap a good harvest."[1] Poverty made the farmers all the more vulnerable to corrupt tax collectors, who preyed upon those least able to resist. Tax collection had become, in fact, a lucrative loan business run from within the local government itself. Clerks of the county office had to meet their collection quotas on time, even if taxpayers were in arrears. So they turned their predicament to profit by advancing the tax payments at usurious interest. These middlemen brought government and commerce together in a combination that was ruinous to the villages.

[1] *Leiyang xianzhi*, 1886 ed., 7:1b. I use "farmer" instead of "peasant," except when quoting sources from the Chinese Communist Party or government.

Far from forbidding the practice, magistrates relied upon it, because their own careers depended on full and timely tax collection. And on the fringes of local government, unpaid (and unregulated) tax agents (*lishu, lichai*) lived on fees extorted from villagers. Particularly onerous were the surtaxes for the Grain Transport Administration, whose costs of collection and transport (including profits for middlemen) had become an intolerable aggravation to the hard-pressed farmers.

The crisis of the 1840s was felt in Leiyang's villages as a shortage of silver, the metal in which the land-tax was paid. Copper, the cash of the common man, had to be transported long distances to the county seat, there to be exchanged for silver. Surtaxes for "meltage" were burdensome enough, but the underlying problem was the value of silver relative to copper. As silver rose in price, the real tax burden soared. Corruption and usury, barely supportable when the currency was stable, now became detonators of rebellion.[2]

Under these intolerable conditions, the farmers turned to the licentiates (*shengyuan*) and holders of purchased studentships (*jiansheng*): the lowest stratum of the rural elite, who undertook to pay their neighbors' taxes by proxy and fend off the tax agents' extortion. Such "proxy remittance"

[2]Internal government documents on the Leiyang uprising are preserved in the First Historical Archives, Beijing. On the origins of the Leiyang rebellion, see reports from the Hunan provincial governor, Lufei Quan, *Zhupi zouzhe nongmin yundong*, 980.03 (11 Jan. 1843), and *Lufu zouzhe nongmin yundong*, 3390–2 (two memorials of 26 Oct., comprising Lufei's judgments on the armed rebellion and on the tax-resistance offenses; and 22 Nov. 1844, his analysis of the abuses in the tax system). On moneylending by tax-collection agents, see *Leiyang xianzhi* 1886, 7–10, a well-informed essay by a retired local official. On "tax fronting" (advance payment by collectors) see Bradly Reed, *Talons and Teeth: County Clerks and Runners in the Qing Dynasty* (Stanford, Calif.: Stanford University Press, 2000), pp. 183ff.

was forbidden by law, but for centuries had been widely practiced. Profit was involved here, too: the lower elite took fees for their trouble.[3] Yet during hard times, the proxy-remittance business of these middlemen served a pressing community need.

Proxy remittance, a chronic practice, was not likely in itself to constitute a political threat to the authorities. Another licentiate activity, however, was more dangerous: filing formal charges against the tax clerks. One Duan Ba-cui, a respected licentiate from a rural lineage, journeyed to Beijing during the winter of 1842 to enter a "capital appeal" (*jingkong*) against the Leiyang clerks. Such capital appeals, though authorized by law, had been an embarrassing nuisance to the court for decades. Beijing ordinarily remanded them to the provincial governors, who could be relied upon to protect their subordinates. Duan's appeal was, in due course, rejected; he was accused of false pleading and was sentenced to be beaten and banished.

Into the Leiyang jail went Duan, in March 1843, to await exile to the frontiers. But now he was in the hands of his mortal enemies, the county clerks, who, it was rumored, were planning to kill him by starvation (a fate common enough for impecunious prisoners). His kinsmen took counsel with Yang Dapeng, a forty-seven-year-old former licentiate who had helped Duan with his original lawsuit. With Yang's advice, they called for a boycott of county examinations. This stratagem, detested by officials, was a

[3]On the social position of licentiates, see Min Tu-ki, *National Polity and Local Power: The Transformation of Late Imperial China* (Cambridge, Mass: Council on East Asian Studies, Harvard University, 1989), pp. 21–49. Yang Dapeng, the leader of the Leiyang revolt, was the registered owner of about enough land for a vegetable plot. *Leiyang xianzhi* 1886, 2:2.

traditional gesture of resistance to oppressive government. The magistrate struck back by arresting Duan's son for posting boycott notices, and scheduled a judicial hearing for March 15.[4] Now the Duans undertook a daring rescue. Along with members of at least four other lineages, a band of Duans filtered into town at dawn on the fifteenth, wrested an unwilling Duan Bacui from his guards, and fled to the countryside.

Other local notables thought they could head off disaster by reasoning with the magistrate. Liang Renwang, who had long been involved in proxy tax remittance, was hated by the clerks whose tax-loan business he threatened.[5] He now led a delegation of members from at least eight lineages to the county offices. Admitted to the magistrate's great hall, Liang accused the tax clerks of extortion and begged that they be dismissed and surtaxes reduced. Liang "feared that if the magistrate did not issue a proclamation as he had requested, the sentiments of the people would no longer be amenable to control."[6] This timely warning of rebellion the magistrate took as extortion. He called for his bailiffs, but the petitioners fled. The tax clerks had hardened the magistrate against him, Liang believed, and the next day he led a group of two dozen men into town to give them a beating. The clerks could not be found, but their houses were sacked, amid general looting. Troops of

[4]*Leiyang xianzhi* 1886, 8:11–12b; Yang had been stripped of licentiate status as a penalty for helping Duan raise funds for his original "false" appeal. See Yang's "confession" after his capture: *Lufu zouzhe, nongmin yundong*, 3390–2 (26 Oct. 1844).

[5]I have not been able to discover whether Liang had licentiate status.

[6]*Lufu zouzhe* 26 Oct. 1844 (on tax resistance and Liang Renwang's appeal to the magistrate). With his son still in jail, Duan Bacui surrendered himself to the governor-general's office in Wuchang, Hubei province, hoping for justice outside his native Hunan.

the county garrison attacked the crowd, leaving the streets littered with bodies; but the ringleaders escaped.[7]

Deep in the countryside, the leaders of tax resistance now began to act as a *de facto* local government. Yang Dapeng, the litigation expert, now turned his hand to raising funds for further legal appeals. During the summer of 1843, he collaborated with heads of local lineages to impose an unofficial tax upon all households in the county. Wealthy lineages of the neighboring Eastern District opened a "bureau" in a local ancestral hall to collect funds and forge weapons. Paid collectors were sent into villages throughout the county. Yang and his coadjutors in the Western District forged a stele of iron, on which were written new "regulations for collecting the land and grain-tribute taxes." The Duan ancestral hall was named "Star of Fortune Collection Office" (*fuxing gongguan*) and designated as a center for collecting funds and issuing receipts.[8] The Yang and Duan lineage leaders "prevented taxpayers from entering the county seat" to pay government taxes. The resulting shortfall in revenues in the summer of 1843 provoked brutal repression. Government troops burned the collection office and arrested its agents (including Yang Dapeng's younger brother).

The arrests pushed the Yang and Duan lineages from tax resistance to armed revolt. In the villages, "the gongs

[7]*Leiyang xianzhi* 1886, 8:11a.
[8]*Zhupi zouzhe* 980.14 (5 Feb. 1845). The term *gongguan* was used euphemistically for a landlord's rent-collecting office (Lin Man-houng, private communication). Historically, however, it clearly meant a government office. Exactly what it meant to its Leiyang leadership in 1844 cannot be stated conclusively. In practice, we know that it was associated with revenue collection and that, although it was situated at a lineage hall, its directorate included more than one lineage.

were sounded," and the assembled farmers were exhorted by their lineage leaders. On July 2, a ragtag army of 400 armed men marched on the county seat to seize the prisoners, only to be driven back by gunfire from the city wall. Urgent notes to the lineages of the Eastern District summoned more recruits. Four great wooden cannon were constructed. Now a crowd numbering more than 1,000, from both Eastern and Western districts, attacked the town repeatedly over the course of two days. Among them was a monk who could "use incantations to stop up the muzzles of guns." But government reinforcements had now arrived from the prefectural seat of Hengzhou, and the rebels were no match for them. Though the sound of their wooden cannon "rent the very rocks of the mountains,"[9] they unfortunately had exploded in their mounts, killing the gunners. The final attack withered under government gunfire, and the rebels fled to the hills.

Government troops now slaughtered and burned their way through the Leiyang hills, but managed to arrest only 225 men. By early August, Yang Dapeng himself had been tracked down. After writing his own confession at the provincial capital, he was sent to Beijing to be executed by "slow slicing."

The official diagnosis of the Leiyang disaster called attention to two endemic maladies of the Qing revenue system: illegal middlemen and faulty tax registers. The middlemen included the county clerks, who were operating with the tacit complicity of the officials themselves; and the licentiates, such as Duan Bacui and Yang Dapeng, who practiced proxy remittance and filed lawsuits against the

---

[9]Feng Guifen, "Leiyang jiwen," in *Xianzhitang ji* 4:36b.

clerks.[10] Of these, the licentiates seemed the more dangerous. Though the clerks parasitized both government and
taxpayers, the licentiates could cut off government revenue
altogether and behave like lords of the countryside. Com-
manding funds, manpower, and a measure of community
respect, these lowly literati appeared darkly threatening.
The licentiates, wrote Governor-general Yutai, were

using the clerks and runners' excess exactions as a pretext for
openly gathering mobs and resisting authority. Surely there are
malpractices in the clerks and runners' management of tax collection. Yet unless these scoundrelly fellows are rigorously punished, we cannot be sure that they will not stir up future inci-
dents.[11]

Logically, the middleman problem had to be dealt with on
both sides—clerks and licentiates—but the clerks were in-
dispensable to the official system, and their malpractices were
left essentially untouched.[12]

Middlemen, whether clerks or licentiates, owed their
positions to the faulty system of tax registration. The tax
system inherited from the Ming dynasty used registers of two
types: cadastres, which showed the amount, the quality,
and the ownership of all taxable land; and household registers, which showed tax liability, for both landtax and labor
service. Under the early Ming *lijia* system, local headmen
performed tax-collection duty as a rotating labor obliga-
tion. By the sixteenth century, however, commercialization

[10]These men correspond to the practitioners of *baoshou* and *baolan* described by
Wang Yeh-chien in *Land Taxation in Imperial China, 1750–1911* (Cambridge, Mass:
Harvard University Press, 1973), p. 42.

[11]Yutai's memorial (980.2) is dated 10 Oct. 1843.

[12]Some of the clerks were punished with beatings and temporary banishment.
Lufu zouzhe, nongmin yundong, 26 Oct. 1844 (on tax resistance).

and population growth had rendered both types of register unreliable. The link between land ownership and residence, which formed the basis of the *lijia* tax system, had been irreparably broken. Beijing tried to keep the system workable by creating tax districts of equal liability, but this measure proved unable to keep up with changes in land ownership and population. Local headmen were dunned for amounts they could not collect, and their families were ruined.

As the Ming system of local headmen became unworkable, the *lijia* units (originally groups of 110 households) came to represent areas of taxable land rather than groups of people. By the 1680s, amounts to be collected from these areas had become purely conventional—and were in fact ordered by imperial decree to be engraved on stone and posted at county offices. There was to be no systematic effort to add newly opened land to the tax registers. Accordingly, the main task in land taxation was *to fix responsibility upon tax collectors for obtaining a conventional sum from known areas of land.* This responsibility reached to the lowest bureaucratic official, the magistrate, but also perforce to his revenue clerks.[13] The difficulties were of two main kinds: as Governor Lufei pointed out in the Leiyang case, those dunned for taxes were not necessarily those who had the resources to pay them; and the fixed tax quotas did not provide for the actual expenses of local government—not even the costs of collection—a situation that necessitated the unauthorized surtaxes so hated by the farmers.

---

[13]The legislative history of Qing land-tax systems can be followed in *Huangchao wenxian tongkao* (Taipei: 1963, Geda shuju reprint of imperially compiled Qianlong edition, n.p. n.d.), *tianfu 2.* The classic accounts of the tax system are Ho Ping-ti, *Studies on the Population of China* (Cambridge, Mass.: Harvard University Press, 1959); and Wang, *Land Taxation in Imperial China.*

Shortfalls in collection, which underlay the clerks' loan business and the licentiates' resistance, were a natural consequence of the chaotic state of the tax registers. Governor Lufei Quan summed up the problem: in a freewheeling market, many taxpayers held fields that appeared in tax registers of other villages. Because the tax collectors were held responsible for coming up with the entire quota for a given area by a certain time, fields whose owners lived elsewhere and could not readily be found were taxed to villagers who lived in that area.[14] As a result, wrote the governor, there are "those who farm fields but pay no taxes on them, and those who pay taxes on fields they do not own."

To fix responsibility on the actual owners, Governor Lufei proposed that tax records be recompiled and keyed to human settlements (that is, by listing both village inhabitants and the fields owned by each, in whatever jurisdiction), and not to cadastres of taxable land. This method he called "controlling land through people" (*yiren tongdi*). "If someone living in one village buys a parcel of taxable land [that is entered in the register of] another village, all the taxes he owes should be entered in one register, and be collected under [the register of] his own village."[15] Such a

---

[14]The practice of holding villagers collectively responsible for taxable acreage in the vicinity of their settlements can be considered the real origin of the "apportioned funds" (*tankuan*) system of the twentieth century, which is discussed later in this essay.

[15]*Lufu zouzhe nongmin yundong*, 3390–2, 22 Nov. 1844 (memorial by Lufei Quan). "*Yiren tongdi*" appears to be another term for the "village-based" system described by Kuribayashi Nobuo in *Rikōsei no kenkyū* (A study of the *lijia* system; Tokyo: Bunri shōin, 1971), pp. 337–46. The new "village-based" (*shunzhuang*) system, in which registers were keyed to place of residence, had been instituted in East-Central China as early as the 1720s, but there is no evidence that it had been applied to Leiyang. This system was an important part of the fiscal rationalization under-

remedy had been used in other jurisdictions as early as the 1720s and was known as the "village-based" (*shunzhuang*) system. The land-owning household, accurately located in its settlement, was to be the point of reference for the purpose of keeping registers up to date. Tax-clerks would be permitted to dun a household for the land it owned anywhere in the county, but could no longer hold villagers responsible for making up the tax due on parcels whose owners were in default or could not be located. This was a reasonable response to the free market in land, the growth of population and cultivated land, and the obsolescence of the old cadastres inherited from the Ming. Nevertheless, to keep such registers up-to-date would have required a formidable output of administrative energy and discipline.

The difficulties of applying Governor Lufei's system can be clarified by comparison with the revenue system of British India. Indian land revenue depended upon two alternative principles of tax collection. The system employed in Bengal used officially recognized middlemen, the *zamindars*, who were administratively descended from a stratum of official tax farmers under the defunct Mughal Empire. Elsewhere, notably in Madras, individual cultivators were responsible directly to the state, with no middlemen in the system. The Madras system, known as *ryotwari* (revenue coming directly from the cultivator or *ryot*) required an assiduous, unending process of "settlement," or assessment of tax due from particular cultivators, to take account of

---

taken by the Yongzheng emperor. The essence of it was to compile registers based on the place of residence of the taxpayers, with each listed household responsible for its taxable acreage in any part of the county. Land owned by households living outside the county boundaries would be listed in a separate register, presumably so that local people would not be charged with taxes due on it.

changes in the amount and location of land they owned. Such periodic "settlement" would have been incumbent upon the tax clerks of Leiyang, under the system recommended by Lufei Quan after the rebellion.[16] Chinese county magistrates were, however, in a situation quite different from that of British district administrators. Magistrates were indeed at their clerks' mercy, because their careers depended upon the timely fulfillment of tax quotas; hence every magistrate found himself a co-conspirator with his clerks. And under conditions that pertained in Leiyang, as in countless other poor counties in China, the clerks had a business interest at stake, which depended on keeping the taxpayers in a condition of debt peonage. In India the conferral of individual proprietary rights by the British left smallholders prey to moneylenders (whose capital was attracted by the loan security of individual landholdings), a dreadful if unintended consequence that the British recognized after it was too late to stop it. In China, by contrast, debt peonage had become, in counties like Leiyang, an integral and even a necessary feature of the revenue system. The moneylenders, who had become the magistrates' essential link to their rural tax base, operated their business right out of government offices.

Fiscal Reform and the Trans-Revolutionary State

Leiyang's was one of numerous uprisings led by licentiates during the 1840s; the rebels' exploding cannon symbolize

[16]Eric Stokes, *The English Utilitarians and India* (Oxford: Clarendon Press, 1959), pp. 21–25.

their futility. Like others of its kind,[17] the rebellion exposed social evils which had festered beneath the surface of rural life during the relatively prosperous decades of the late eighteenth century, but which revealed their true malignancy during the economic crisis of the nineteenth. The government response to such uprisings shows that Qing provincial administrators understood their social and institutional origins.

The most ardent reformers of the day, including Wei Yuan, considered that the Leiyang rebellion confirmed everything they had been saying about the ills of the grain tribute system, particularly the opportunities it presented to predatory middlemen. The tax clerks, Wei wrote, "wore caps of office yet behaved like tigers . . . treating the people as their fish and meat." But as self-proclaimed middlemen, the licentiates were no better. The vicious feuds between these rival groups of profiteers were eroding official control over village society.[18] Feng Guifen, too, mistrusted licentiates as middlemen in local society, though he also knew that the Leiyang uprising had really resulted from misgovernment.[19] Both men placed the problem of controlling or eliminating middlemen near the top of China's constitutional agenda. It was an agenda item that was to confront every Chinese government thereafter.

⌒

But why introduce a discussion of collectivized agriculture with a nineteenth-century tax rebellion? It may be objected

---

[17]For documentation of a similar case, see Philip A. Kuhn and John K. Fairbank, *Introduction to Ch'ing Documents: The Rebellion of Chung Jen-chieh* (Cambridge, Mass: Harvard-Yenching Institute, 1993).

[18]Wei Yuan, "Hubei Chongyangxian zhixian Shijun muzhiming," WYJ, p. 338.

[19]Feng Guifen, "Leiyang jiwen," *Xianzhitang ji* 4:36–37.

that between the world of the Leiyang rebellion and the world of the People's Commune, a revolution intervened. Yet revolution changes some things more than others. My inquiry is inspired by the theme of Alexis de Tocqueville's *L'Ancien Régime et la Révolution*: the Old Regime prepared the ground for the new; and although China's revolution wrought many changes, its constitutional agenda reflected some basic concerns of the late imperial and Republican states. Tocqueville's history pictures a long-persisting French state with a history that precedes the Revolution and also survives it. May we, similarly, speak of a "Chinese state" that took shape during the late empire and survived the revolution of 1949? What constitutional issues, and what governmental policies, bridged the gap between the old regime and the new? Our inquiry will focus on the state's long-continued effort to deal with the kind of fiscal malfunction that surfaced in the Leiyang case.

There is some justification here for evoking the Tocquevillian paradigm of a continuous state agenda. Both Bourbon France and late imperial China were regimes incompletely centralized and bureaucratized. In France, some royal administrative posts became the private property of their incumbents (that is, salable or inheritable); this resembles the condition of the Chinese sub-bureaucracy, or clerkdom, in which the commercialization of government is most clearly visible. Yet Tocqueville insists that, despite its relative imperfections by modern standards, the old monarchic system had effectively taken government away from feudal authorities and had achieved the essence of centralized bureaucratic rule. The "modern" bureaucratic state of his day was simply a purer form of what the Old Regime had accomplished, "once all that had grown up around it had been cut away."[20] For Tocqueville, the Old Regime was a centralized bureaucracy imperfectly realized. Tocqueville implies that, for the administrative development of the modern state, the French Revolution was not really necessary. Yet the eighteenth-century French state was even further from a bureaucracy than Tocqueville supposed. The centralization he described did not involve a true career administration; nor had it yet evinced that vital element of bureaucracy, the separation of private from public funds, because so much public money was handled by the *financiers* as a business. In the words of one authority, the centralized bureaux of the Old Regime were actually "a combination of aristocracy and private business."[21] From this combination grew the French government's fiscal weakness on the eve of revolution. For the revolutionary and then the Napoleonic state to combat aristocracy and privilege meant installing a new principle of public service for more efficient tax collection.

Although Tocqueville was surely right that the modern French state did not build bureaucracy upon thin air, he perhaps underrated the function of revolution in destroy-

---

[20]Alexis de Tocqueville, *L'Ancien Régime et la Révolution* (Paris: Gallimard, 1967), p. 128.

[21]John Francis Bosher, *French Finances 1770–1795: From Business to Bureaucracy* (Cambridge, Eng: Cambridge University Press, 1970), p. 276. The difference between gross and net taxation managed by the *fermiers générales* was probably at least 20 percent, including profit and cost of collection. See Peter Mathias and Patrick O'Brien, "Taxation in Britain and France 1715–1810: A Comparison of the Social and Economic Incidence of Taxes Collected for the Central Governments," *Journal of European Economic History* (1976), 645–46. The commercial element in public finance made the late-eighteenth-century French monarchy "more a client than the master of financial agencies." Wolfram Fischer and Peter Lundgreen, "The Recruitment and Training of Administrative and Technical Personnel," in Tilly, ed., *The Formation of National States in Western Europe* (Princeton, N.J.: Princeton University Press, 1975), p. 496.

ing those elements of commerce and privilege that made the late Bourbon fiscal system so expensive to the taxpayers yet so unproductive for the state. Although I shall argue that in China, too, the Old Regime had prepared the way for the new, I should not like to underestimate the force of the revolution in "cutting away" commerce and privilege from the fiscal system. In the French case, as in the Chinese, something fundamental had to happen to the social system before there could be constitutional change in the state.[22]

Save at its lowest levels, the Chinese government did not farm out the power to tax, in the sense of rendering that power purchasable ("venal" in the French sense) or leasable. Instead, Chinese monarchs had to cope with a deeply ingrained "prebendal" political culture, to use Max Weber's term. Although a provincial governor or county magistrate did not "own" his post, he did have what amounted to a royal license to tax. He received (after the 1720s) a not inconsiderable salary, but far from enough to maintain his family and official staff. Officials therefore had to forage for themselves, passing on to the center only explicitly mandated quotas and keeping the rest.[23] Here was the basis of a field administration that was seemingly frugal, but, from the taxpayers' point of view, actually quite expensive. And as commerce suffused the lower rungs of

[22]In rejecting the idea that French administration had been decisively bureaucratized by 1789, Clive Church insists that there was "a point beyond which reform could not go without a change in the nature of 'domination,' as Weber would say." "The Process of Bureaucratization in France, 1789–1799," *Die Französische Revolution—zufälliges oder notwendiges Ereignis?* (Munich: Oldenbourg Verlag GmbH, 1983), vol. 1, p. 126.

[23]On this subject see Madeleine Zelin, *The Magistrate's Tael: Rationalizing Fiscal Reform in Eighteenth-Century Ch'ing China* (Berkeley: University of California Press, 1984), especially Chap. 2.

the system (county government and its clerkly usurers), the nineteenth-century state faced a vexing anomaly: the farmers were up in arms against extortionate taxes, while the state's revenues remained short of its needs—a situation not dissimilar from the France of Louis XVI.[24]

Since its conquest of China in 1644, the Qing regime had been intent on protecting its agricultural tax from the intrusion of middlemen. In the early Qing period, official reports associated "proxy remittance" (*baolan*) with the venerable practice of "false registration" (*guiji*), by which commoners' lands were sheltered from taxation under the name of a privileged local magnate. Such practices, though forbidden under the criminal code inherited from the Ming, were increasingly common in the eighteenth century.

The fiscal policy of the Manchu ruling house had been

[24]How commercialized was the bureaucracy itself? At least some contemporaries saw the spirit of commerce reaching well beyond the lowly clerks and into the upper elite. Consider the following passage from the seventeenth-century writer Gu Yanwu: "The superior man does not personally involve himself with giving gifts [to superior officials]. In antiquity, the reason the gifts of silk were wrapped in paper and presented in bamboo boxes [referring here to the *Ode* "Deer Call"] is not merely to decorate them appropriately, but also to foster the mental habit of distancing oneself from wealth and nourishing a sense of shame. Since the Wanli reign [1573–1620], when great officials got together, they mostly used silver [as gifts]. But they [still] concealed it between the leaves of books. They would present it through the intermediacy of the doorkeeper. Now, however [i.e., in the early Qing period, late seventeenth century], they simply . . . take the silver directly from their bosoms, and do not pass it through a third party. Their chit-chat is solely about the money. Official robes and caps are the place to repose one's purse [i.e., invest one's money]; the court and the government offices have taken on the appearance of a market." *Huangchao jingshi wenbian* 3:2b–3. Although bureaucratic posts were not for sale, it is clear that commercialism had already crept into the system by the late Ming period. In fact, the government had only encouraged its own commercialization since the eighteenth century by periodically putting academic titles and even official posts on sale. These practices had become a public scandal by the end of the nineteenth century.

to keep the tax burden light, while cowing landowning elites who might insert themselves between the state and the farmer. As middlemen, big landlords were potentially the most damaging to dynastic interests. Along with a number of measures that favored the interests of small-holders (presumably more docile taxpayers), the regime cracked down hard on major tax evaders.[25] The Manchus, as outsiders, were not beholden to the landed elites in China's richest provinces, particularly the area of the Yangzi River delta, and in fiscal matters could treat them ruthlessly. In 1661 thousands of prominent land-owning gentry were punished (some even jailed or beaten) for tax evasion. However, tax prosecutions of the extent and violence of 1661 were not repeated, and tax evasion actually went from bad to worse thereafter. Under the relatively lenient rule of Kangxi (1662–1722) the penalties to be inflicted were gradually reduced, especially for the upper elite. By the early eighteenth century, elite tax evasion had become a pervasive part of the local scene. To avoid trouble with local notables, magistrates customarily hid their defalcations under the general heading of "taxpayer deficits" (*minqian*).

By the 1720s, Beijing had become so alarmed about the loss of revenue to proxy-remittance middlemen that the Yongzheng emperor resolved to put an end to the elite's ability to shield others' land. His attention was drawn particularly to tax-meddling by the lower elite. Licentiates, he complained, were representing themselves as "scholar households" (or "official households" if they had purchased the

---

[25]On early Qing tax policies, see Liu Cuirong, "Qingchu Shunzhi Kangxi nianjian jianmien fushui di guocheng, in " Zhou Kangxie, ed., *Zhongguo jin sanbainian jingjishi lunji*, 2 vols. (Hong Kong: Chongwen shuju, 1972), vol. 1, pp. 13–33.

jiansheng degree) and were collecting the taxes of lower-status kinsmen. Beginning in 1726, a barrage of royal edicts decreed ruinous penalties for proxy remitters. Stiffer penalties were announced for tax evaders, even doctorate holders (*jinshi*) and retired officials. Yet an energetic investigation of the usual suspects, the rich Jiangnan elites, yielded few prosecutions. By 1732 Yongzheng had to back down, after discovering how widespread tax evasion had become among the local elite, and how little local officials were willing to do about it. On the upper levels of elite status, *de facto* tax immunity simply served to protect private wealth. On the lower levels (the licentiates), such immunity made possible the commercial enterprise of proxy remittance. Yongzheng's less rigorous successor kept severe penalties on the books; yet elite meddling in the tax system proved impossible to stamp out. It was the undiminished ability of the elite to evade taxes that made them ideal middlemen from the farmer's point of view. For the smallholder, the mandated "self-delivery" of taxes (mandated in some areas since the 1530s—a kind of *ryotwari* system) was cumbersome and costly, and dealing directly with the clerk-runner tax agents could be ruinous. Men of higher status (such as the licentiates who made a business of proxy remittance) were convenient buffers, even necessary ones, between the farmer and the state.[26]

Yet if Yongzheng had known what would follow a cen-

---

[26]*Da Qing huidian shili* (Taipei: Zhongwen shuju; 1963 reprint of Guangxu edition), 172.18b–19. This subject is treated authoritatively in Yamamoto Eishi, "Yōsei shinkin kōryō shobun kō," *Chūgoku kindaishi kenkyū* 7 (July 1992), pp. 78–115; and "Shinkin ni yoru suiryō hōran to Shinchō kokka," *Tōyōshi kenkyū* 48.4 (March 1990), pp. 40–69. See Xue Yunsheng, *Duli cunyi* (Taipei: Chinese Materials Center, 1970), 2.328, for the proxy remittance statute. Yongzheng's substatute aimed at elite defaulters is on 2.324.

tury later, his forebodings about local tax middlemen would have seemed hardly bleak enough; for the economic crisis of the early nineteenth century transformed what had been primarily a fiscal menace into a political one. Where Yongzheng in the 1720s had seen proxy remittance as a threat to the state's revenue, his great-grandson Daoguang in the 1840s saw it as a threat to dynastic control. Middlemen, whose activities depended on the ill-adjusted relationship between settlement and taxable land, were now leaders of armed rebellion.

What was to be done? Cases like Leiyang showed that the Qing authorities understood how the commercialization of government had affected tax collection in the counties. But under the circumstances, not much could be done about the underlying causes. Although clerks and runners were recognized as a pervasive evil, permitting the likes of Yang Dapeng to control local society was not an acceptable solution; and armed repression was the inevitable result. To have local notables leading armed bands of farmers and levying their own irregular taxes seemed, reasonably enough, a prelude to disaster.

Yet historic circumstances soon changed the court's view of the matter. Only a decade after Yang Dapeng's severed head was hung on display in December 1844, "to warn the masses," the court found itself patronizing locally led and locally financed militia corps, all over central China, that probably differed little from Yang's organization in Leiyang. The compelling reason was the defense of the established order against the Taiping Rebellion. Local militia leaders now raised armed bands and supported them through irregular surtaxes upon the land. What had been unthinkable in the Leiyang case had become a condition for resisting the regime's enemies.

Nevertheless, even under such desperate conditions, we can observe the state attempting to limit the fiscal damage. Leadership was taken by the scholar-generals whose armies now stood between the Taiping rebels and the Qing monarchy, and whose immediate aim was to raise funds for their own armies. The situation in the middle-Yangzi province of Hubei offers an example. Even as his army grappled with the Taiping rebels, Governor Hu Linyi instituted a province-wide tax reform. Reducing the state's demands would encourage landowners to pay their taxes in full, and new registers would fix liability more effectively. The key (in keeping with long-term Qing fiscal policy) was to link landownership firmly to residence. Every plot was to be ascribed to a person who resided in the same tax district. To drive out middlemen, the reform would impose a cap on the "surtaxes" by which their commercial enterprises had thrived. Reliable local literati would manage tax collection in their place.[27]

These and other fiscal reforms of the moribund empire proved largely ineffective.[28] The "prebendal" character of the official system and the commercialization of local government were too deeply ingrained. But futile as they proved in the short run, such reforms show that the mid-

[27]William T. Rowe, "Hu Lin-i's Reform of the Grain Tribute System in Hupeh, 1855–1858," *Ch'ing-shih wen-t'i* 4.10 (Dec. 1983), pp. 33–86. The originator of efforts to reform the tax system in the middle-Yangzi provinces was Luo Bingzhang, Governor of Hunan. Wang Yeh-chien, *Land Taxation*, p. 35.

[28]For a report on the backsliding in Hubei, see a memorial by Tu Renshou dated 11 May 1884, in Wang Xianqian, *Guangxuchao donghualu* (Shanghai, 1909; reprint: Beijing, 1984), 11 May 1884 (Tu Renshou), p. 1701.

dleman problem and the fiscal linkage between land and residence remained high on the agenda of the Old Regime.

Fiscal Reform and State-Building in the Twentieth Century

In the aftermath of China's humiliation during the Boxer Rebellion, the imperial government faced two urgent tasks: to extract more revenue from rural society to pay the huge indemnities demanded by the Western powers and to modernize China's armies; and to give the dynasty a new lease on life by setting up a constitutional system in imitation of Japan. Both tasks required new approaches to local taxation.

The constitutional reforms of the first decade of the twentieth century established a local tax base for the first time. Merchants and literati who participated in the "local self-government" of the 1900s obtained the power to tax their own communities for projects such as Western-style police and schools (to name only the most expensive items). For local elites, here was a chance to wrest fiscal authority from their old enemies, the subbureaucracy of county clerks. From the viewpoint of the state, however, "local self-government" turned out to be an annoying competitor for revenue. From the very first years of the Republic, the regular bureaucracy strove to reestablish its own control over local taxes. Under the Nanjing government of Chiang Kai-shek, provincial authorities did their best to drive local elites out of the taxation system. Indeed, Nanjing's campaign against "local bullies and evil gentry" (men perhaps not very different from Yang Dapeng in Leiyang) was presented in populist rhetoric, but is most plausibly

understood as a step toward firmer control over the revenue of the countryside. Besides asserting control over local
elites, Nanjing (and the Japanese occupiers who followed
them) energetically pushed local government deeper into
the countryside. Between county town and rural village
were inserted new administrative units, which were even-
tually standardized at roughly the scale of the market-com-
munity, and known as townships (*xiang*).[29]

Bringing the tax system back under bureaucratic control
was the part of state-making most firmly rooted in the
agenda of the Old Regime. The fiscal history of the Republic, however, is not so much a story of consolidation as
of expansion. Just as warfare had played a part in European
state-making, the chaotic years of Republican China drove
governments to extract more of the farmer's surplus production to supply their expanding armies.

The most hated of the new taxes was levied by warlord
regimes of doubtful legitimacy: the new, *ad hoc* tax known
as "apportioned funds" (*tankuan*). Lacking reliable registers of taxable land, authorities simply required a village to
pay a certain sum, leaving it to the local headman to "apportion" the payments. This onerous system had the effect
of linking settlements and taxable land, because a village
now needed a well-defined boundary to demarcate taxable
fields within its control. The *tankuan* also had political
consequences: as a result of his power to apportion taxes,
the village head assumed a more prominent role in local
government.[30]

[29]The outstanding account of this process is Prasenjit Duara, *Culture, Power, and the State: Rural North China, 1900–1942* (Stanford, Calif.: Stanford University Press, 1988) pp. 58–85.

[30]Ibid., pp. 71ff.

When Mao Zedong mounted Tiananmen to declare that the Old Regime was finally dead, his government was thus already the heir to certain innovations of the Republican period, including the finer mesh of subcounty government left by the Guomindang, and the administrative practice of linking land with settlement in a format of bounded villages. Looking further back, we can see how all twentieth-century regimes had inherited the old monarchic ambition to drive unauthorized middlemen out of the tax system. We must now consider in detail where collectivization fits into this process of administrative evolution.

∽

Underlying collectivization can be seen the urgent priorities of the modern Chinese state. These were defined by the intersecting requirements of agricultural revenue and industrialization. Collectivization offered a new method of relating them. The revenue problem faced by the New Regime can be understood in two aspects. First was the familiar challenge of maintaining access to the farmers' surplus production, unimpeded by predatory or protective middlemen. Second was a problem largely ignored by earlier twentieth-century regimes: the task of actually raising agricultural production, whether through capital inputs or social reorganization.

Of rural middlemen the revolutionaries had long been sworn enemies. Like the imperial and republican governments before them, the Communists considered them oppressors of the farmers and a menace to the state. Now they were defined in the rhetoric of class exploitation, and little was said about them as impediments to revenue collection. But that was a question which no state, especially an industrializing one, could long ignore.

By 1952, the process of "land reform" was complete. Landlords and rich farmers had had their land taken away and distributed among the landless. A vast new stratum of smallholders was thereby created, termed optimistically "new middle peasants," though most got barely enough acreage for subsistence. An essential part of land reform was to destroy local elites as an economic and political force, often by killing them. For the most part, however, the rural elites affected by land reform were not large rentiers (most of whom were urbanized absentees), but rich farmers who hired some labor or rented out some land. Many were also petty rural administrators: village headmen who had served the old regime as tax collectors, and who can hardly be regarded as "landlords." As a political measure, land reform eliminated a class of state agents whose own "take" had kept much tax revenue from reaching the state. The Communist Party replaced them with men drawn from the poorest stratum of farmers, men who owed everything to the Communist Party and were therefore both sympathetic to the new regime and readily controllable by it.

Because the "new middle peasants" lacked sufficient land, tools, and draft animals to farm effectively, the new regime quickly organized groups of households into "mutual-aid teams," to share tools and labor. The immediate task was economic recovery. Though collectivization was an ultimate goal, it seemed to lie far in the future. As the village economy began to revive, however, some old political problems began to alarm provincial authorities: inequalities of wealth were reappearing, and a new class of "rich peasants" seemed likely to emerge as competitors for control of village China and its agricultural surplus. The problem was first perceived in Shanxi province, an area in North China that had long been under Communist control. The provincial Party committee warned, in April 1951, that mutual-aid teams were actually being weakened by the economic recovery. The farmers were not following "in the direction of the modernization and collectivization that we demand, but in the direction of a rich peasantry." If this trend continued, the results would be either that the mutual-aid teams would disband, or that they would become "the manorial estates of the rich peasants." Party control was weakening, as formerly poor rural cadres became "rich peasants" themselves. The provincial Party committee proposed to begin collectivization promptly and thereby "shake, weaken, and ultimately disestablish" private ownership.[31]

The Shanxi problem appeared initially as one of state access to the agricultural surplus—the viewpoint of local officials, and essentially a problem shared with the Old Regime. But at the uppermost levels of the Party, the question was debated on grounds of production. In this respect, the Shanxi case offers a revealing glimpse of future events. Dismissing the Shanxi proposal as premature, Mao's top lieutenants insisted that, at this early stage of China's economic development, increased production still depended on the private energies of the most efficient

[31]Original documents on collectivization are printed in *Nongye jitihua zhongyang wenjian huibian* (Collected Central Committee documents on agricultural collectivization), which includes previously unpublished material from Central Committee files. Beijing: Zhongyang dangxiao (Central Party School), 2 vols., 1981. For internal circulation (referred to hereafter as HB). For the Shanxi case, see vol. I, pp. 35–36. A proposal of the Shanxi Provincial Party Committee, 17 April 1951. Bo Yibo, *Ruogan zhongda jueci yu shijian di huigu* (Beijing, 1991) vol. I, pp. 184–211.

farmers, and that it was accordingly too early to do away with private landownership. But Mao overruled them, and the Party began to expand collectivization in earnest in December 1953. Mao's position was powerfully reinforced, among Party leaders, by Stalin's successor, Malenkov, who was busily touting the supposed success of Soviet collective agriculture.[32]

China's collectivization, however, was occurring amid desperate problems in supplying the cities. To procure urban grain supplies, Beijing had relied on market purchase more than upon the agricultural tax. But as demand forced grain prices up, new solutions had to be found. Here we can see how the Old Regime's revenue problems were being transformed by modern conditions. The rapid growth of the industrial work force was putting heavy pressure on state grain supplies. A decision in 1953 to stabilize the amounts of grain collected through taxes meant that all increases in demand would have to be met by market purchase, in competition with private merchants. Under these conditions, demand drove grain prices ever higher. To ensure a supply of cheap grain for the cities, the leadership instituted, in late 1953, a system of compulsory grain purchase, in mandated amounts and at fixed prices. This system had originally been discussed under the name "compulsory purchase" (*zhenggou*), but because the term had been current during the Japanese occupation, the less intimidating "unified purchase" (*tonggou*) was substituted.[33] The private market in agricultural products was abolished; both purchase and sales were now handled by government agencies.

[32]Bo Yibo, vol. I, p. 363.
[33]Ibid., p. 266.

"Unified purchase" was a significant step in the history of Chinese taxation. It was indeed a blow against middlemen. But it went beyond ensuring the State's share of the surplus to actually increasing that share. It was not simply a matter of mandating grain prices, but also of mandating amounts. It was therefore a powerful extraction device, though it was never publicly acknowledged to be a tax.[34] The enhancement of the state's revenue amounted to what it appropriated from the farmers (through the mandated low purchase price), plus what extra amounts it could squeeze from them by, in effect, limiting how much of their own produce they could eat.

What "unified purchase" could not do, however, was to actually increase production. And dividing a slowly growing agricultural surplus between the farmers and a rapidly growing urban workforce was not a likely basis for a modern industrial nation. Mao believed that the difference would be made by collectivization. What the West had achieved through the slow accumulation of capital would be achieved rapidly in China through collective management and mass indoctrination.

In October 1953, Mao warned that private ownership in agriculture was "totally in conflict with large-scale supply." Collectivization would be an essential precondition for "raising productive power and completing the country's industrialization."[35] Two years later, on the brink of rapid collectivization, Mao denounced those in the Party who

---

[34]This ambiguity is not unlike the practice known as "harmonious purchase" (*hedi*) in the late Tang and Song periods (eighth to thirteenth centuries), which aimed, in principle, to fill up local granaries, and which was often denounced as a tax in disguise.

[35]"Talks on Agricultural Mutual-Aid and Cooperativization," HB, vol. 1, p. 199.

advocated a slow, cautious approach:

They do not know that socialist industrialization cannot proceed independently, separately from agricultural cooperativization. Our nation has a very low level of production in commercial grain and industrial raw materials. But the state's needs for these products is rising year by year. This is a contradiction.

If collectivization could not be achieved within three five-year plans, "then our socialist industrialization could run into the greatest difficulty."[36]

By the autumn of 1955, Mao had convinced or intimidated the Party into accepting the proposition that only rapid collectivization could support industrial growth. But what was the connection between collectivization and the "unified purchase" system? Here I believe is a way to understand the link to the constitutional problems of the Old Regime. The unit of taxation, including principally "unified purchase," was the collective. In the words of Bo Yibo, one of the architects of the revenue system:

With respect to foodstuffs, the state no longer had any direct relationship with the individual household. The number of taxable units was reduced: from the original figure of more than a hundred million actual households, to a figure of several hundred thousand collectives. This arrangement facilitated the speed of tax collection, the procedures for purchase and supply, and the arrangement of advanced contracts for purchase.[37]

---

[36]"On Agricultural Cooperativization," HB, vol. 1, p. 369. Mao uses the word "cooperativization" (*hezuohua*), but by this time the meaning was what is now referred to as "collectivization" (*jitihua*).

[37]Bo Yibo, vol. I, p. 277. In support of this interpretation, see Jin Guantao and Liu Qingfeng, "Zhongguo gongchandang weishemma fangqi xinminzhu zhuyi?" *Ershiyi shiji shuangyue kan* (Oct. 1992), pp. 13–25, a reference for which I am indebted to Chen Yung-fa.

The chiefs of the collectives became the state's tax agents in the countryside. The social units over which they presided would in certain respects have seemed quite ideal to reform-minded imperial mandarins. Land and residence were now linked in what were in effect bounded villages, and there was no question of determining the tax responsibility for millions of little fields. Tax records were not confused by land transfer, which was now impossible. And finally, the market system was all but obliterated.

Unfortunately for China, this highly effective system of extraction worked great harm during the Great Leap Forward, launched in 1958. With this machinery in place, the regime's utopian overestimate of production led to ruinous grain demands and widespread famine. Though we are assured by one authority that excessive grain procurement during the Great Leap was a result of mistakes, not malice, and that Mao was no Stalin, to a starving farmer the difference may have seemed less salient. Once the machinery was in place, its extractive power could be as cruelly used by a utopian fanatic as by a paranoid murderer.[38]

In any event, the effects of these misfortunes upon the administrative system were profound. In many areas, cadres had reacted to the famine by dismantling collective agriculture entirely and turning over the land to individual families. But the Party was not prepared to give up state control over the village economy. During the retrenchment of the early 1960s, the unit of collective ownership and accounting was now simply reduced to the scale of a neighborhood or a small village, a level at which farmers could

[38]Thomas P. Bernstein, "Stalinism, Famine, and Chinese Farmers: Grain Procurements during the Great Leap Forward," *Theory and Society* 13.3 (1984), pp. 339–77.

see the results of their labor reflected in their earnings, yet land was still bounded and still collective.

The state (now dominated by Liu Shaoqi) considered that the most important political goal of retrenchment was to extend government more effectively into the countryside. In some areas, the chaos that followed the Great Leap had made tax collection all but impossible, because many collectives had simply dissolved. "The state has to collect household by household," complained one provincial official, which was not only administratively troublesome, but also "heightened the contradiction between state and peasantry" (that is, enraged the hungry farmers against the government).[39]

The solution was to transform the larger units of socialist ownership (the communes and the production brigades) into administrative and social service units. In effect, this meant the penetration of civil government to the scale of the large village, a level that the imperial state had left to poorly controlled local elites and tax farmers. Though it remained politically correct to say that the people's commune was "still an integral unit of the collective economy," it was in fact stripped of the most important asset, the ownership of land. Run by a paid state appointee from another area, the people's commune, as an administrative agency roughly on the scale of the old township (*xiang*) of Republican days, was a reliable instrument of state control below the level of the county. Although the local government of Guomindang days had indeed extended its control beneath county level, its effective bureaucratic reach was

[39]HB, vol. 2, p. 561. Resolution of the Anhui Provincial Party Committee, 20 March 1962.

only to the level of the ward (*qu*), a unit much larger than the township. Thus the bureaucratization of the township during the 1960s amounted to a substantial extension of state control.

Retrenchment after the Great Leap thus blended small-scale socialism with intensified bureaucratic control. The system was formalized in a kind of constitutional document, the "Sixty Articles" of 1962, which was to define the essentials of China's rural order for the next seventeen years. The administrative effect of land reform and collectivization was, in simplest terms, a deeper state penetration into village society and a more rigorous system of extraction from it.

The resurgent Maoist radicalism of the mid- and late-1960s once again made the people's commune a powerful force in the economic life of China's villages. Yet the retrenchment and bureaucratization of the early 1960s, as I have just described them, turned out to be the wave of the future. By 1983, Deng Xiaoping had confirmed the separation of township administration from the rural economy. Bureaucratic penetration had survived, even as socialism disintegrated.[40]

The collective system was designed to gather the produce of the weary Chinese farmers more firmly than ever into the hands of the state. The Old Regime's concern with forging an unmediated link to the rural producers had certainly provided the historical foundations of the collectivist experiment. How to control middlemen or put them out of business, how to fix responsibility for tax payment upon human settlements — these were questions the New Regime

---

[40]Robert Ash, "The Evolution of Agricultural Policy," *The China Quarterly* 116 (Dec. 1988), pp. 529–55.

dealt with in revolutionary ways. But if Old and New regimes shared an agenda, does this define away the significance of "revolution?" Surely it does not, as the disasters of the Great Leap Forward demonstrated. Revolution gave the *coup de grace* to the old high culture, which had already been fatally weakened by Western influence and the decline of the old system of elite certification. If the Manchus had owed little to the old landlord elites in their day, the Communists owed nothing whatever. The new system was imposed on a countryside stripped of effective elite leadership. More important, though, was the revolutionary state's commitment to industrialization. The demands of the new state exceeded anything imaginable under the Old Regime, even in the days of the Guomindang. The days when the state sought only a stable maintenance were gone forever. The strategy of squeezing the farmers to bring about forced-draft industrialization, and the administrative power actually to do so, were developments inconceivable without the revolution.

But why was socialism so relatively short-lived a feature of China's rural revolution, and bureaucratic penetration so persistent? Collective agriculture amalgamated the statist fiscal agenda of the Old Regime with the millenarian visions of Mao's later years. This curious amalgam gave Mao's collectivism an appearance that, in retrospect, seems peculiarly archaic.

This archaism can be illustrated by what the anthropologist Fei Xiaotong discovered when in 1957 he revisited his old field-site in Jiangsu. There he found the rural silk industry in ruins. The destruction of the marketing system, along with the Maoist policy of community self-sufficiency in grain, had actually lowered household incomes.[41] For more than two centuries the intricate rural marketing system had enabled Chinese society to adapt to population growth and land shortage. For millions of land-poor Chinese families, crop specialization, market production, and labor export had meant the difference between survival and destitution. The closed, self-sufficient community was a vision common enough in ancient Chinese political thought, but it was radically out of touch with modern realities.

Lest my emphasis on the fiscal-historical roots of collectivization seem a bit monocausal, let me assure the reader that my intent is simply to show how an old agenda can express itself in a new context by stressing the deep structure underlying the modern and the late-imperial Chinese scenes. Collectivization was not "just another Chinese government trying to enhance its revenues by suppressing middlemen." It was an illustration of how that old imperative operated *in a particular context*: one of ideologically driven social engineering to furnish resources for an industrializing economy. That social engineering was, assuredly, fashioned on a revolutionary Marxist-Leninist template of class struggle and the socialization of agriculture. In this context, Mao perceived how the developing Shanxi situation (and others, no doubt, to be expected elsewhere) stood in the way of achieving those historical tasks; but it was his knowledge of Chinese social realities that told him why this was so. The Shanxi "rich peasant" problem must have seemed ominously familiar from his intimate knowledge of how rural society worked. It was not just a matter of "rich

[41]Tomoko Sazanami, "Fei Xiaotong's 1957 Critique of Agricultural Collectivization in a Chinese Village," *Papers on Chinese History* 2 (1993), Fairbank Center, Harvard University, pp. 19–32.

peasants" becoming a new exploiting class, but also of their becoming rivals of the Party for control of the farmers and their surplus production. Mao must also have known how deep were the historical roots of that paradigm, which was certainly in evidence during his village boyhood in the late Qing period. So underneath the practical and ideological imperatives of his own age, Mao found himself dealing with a modern version of a very old agenda.

CHAPTER 4

The Transformation of the
Constitutional Agenda

The literati reaction against Heshen (after he was safely in his grave) was a flurry of activism that Zeng Guofan, writing fifty years later, likened to "a flock of wild ducks taking wing."[1] So contemptuous a judgment seems a bit unfair, when one considers that the man who broke the silence (the Hanlin academician Hong Liangji, 1746–1809) nearly paid with his life. In September 1799, seven months after Heshen's death, Hong had written a detailed indictment—not of Heshen himself, but of the official laxity and cowardice that had permitted him to get so far, and implicitly of the new monarch himself for having failed to press reform. The slack and corrupt administration of the age, which had pro-

---

[1]Zeng Guofan, "Yingzhao chenyan shu" (13 Apr. 1850), *Zeng wenzheng gong quanji* (Taipei: Shijie shuju, 1965), vol. II, pp. 3–5. The main point of Zeng's famous memorial to the newly enthroned Xianfeng was that the late Daoguang emperor had been forced to clamp down on activist bureaucratic factions "in order to change their presumptuous ways" (referring evidently to the repressive hegemony of Grand Councillor Muzhang'a after the Opium War); but that this repression had made officials so timid as to preclude vigorous and effective government.

voked widespread rebellion, had resulted not just from the tyranny of a single "powerful official," but from the apathy of the mass of officials. Participation in high policy was too narrow and too timid, because the monarch himself had failed to seek opinions broadly among officialdom. Few officials either cared or dared to stick their necks out. Worse, because the Jiaqing emperor had done nothing to weed out unworthy officials or to reform the closed political system by which Heshen had usurped executive power, "in the event that a similar despot were to arise, all the officials would again gather at his gate." For his bold, personal criticism, Hong was sentenced to decapitation; but Jiaqing commuted the sentence to banishment. Burdened with a bad conscience, he later pardoned Hong in hopes of obtaining Heaven's favor to end a drought.[2]

We can call Hong's initiative "constitutional" because it criticized existing restraints upon the expression of bureaucratic opinion—and called directly for a more active official elite as a counterweight against despotic power. Yet, for Hong, everything depended on the leadership of the throne: "The spirit of the scholars depends on the sovereign to arouse it."[3] Despotism was to be countered by the integration of the elite and the ruler, not by their opposition.

Though Hong's sense of the integration between elite

[2]The leading study, which includes a translation of Hong's letter, is Susan Mann Jones, "Hung Liang-chi (1746–1809): The Perception and Articulation of Political Problems in Late Eighteenth-Century China" (Stanford University, Ph.D. diss., 1972), pp. 162, 165, 170. See also *Qing shigao* (Beijing: Zhonghua shuju, 1977), 356:11310–11. On the opposition to Heshen, see David S. Nivison, "Ho-shen and His Accusers: Ideology and Political Behavior in the Eighteenth Century," in Nivison and Arthur F. Wright, eds., *Confucianism in Action* (Stanford, Calif.: Stanford University Press, 1959), p. 242.

[3]*Qing shigao*, 356:11311.

and ruler was shared by Wei Yuan, Hong's instinct for martyrdom was not. Reformer-activists of Wei Yuan's generation focused on practical problems of government: "statecraft" was their banner, not constitutional change. Literati
activism, as it developed, addressed itself to many of the
prevailing ills in Chinese life, including the worsening economic crisis in the countryside. Yet the writings of Wei
Yuan, champion of "statecraft," indicate that the constitutional problem lay not far beneath the surface of practical
reform. To cure the ills of the age—particularly the economic crisis that ravaged the countryside—was believed to
require broader involvement by the literate elite. But how
much broader? And by what principle could such involvement avoid being labeled "factional," the kiss of death for
political activism?

Wei Yuan offered his readers classical sanctions for the
idea that the entirety of the elite group he called "*shi*" ought
to play a role in national politics. We have seen that Wei
equated the *shi* with what I have called "established literati"
(that is, those who held a provincial-level degree and, by virtue of their regular gathering in Beijing, could be termed a
national out-of-office elite). The idea that even out-of-office
literati might express themselves on national issues was
quite radical for its time. Yet it already had some practical
basis, notably the employment of established literati (men
like Wei Yuan himself) on the staffs of provincial officials.
These were honorable positions, and their incumbents were
treated as social equals by their official employers. Their position relied on the aspect of elite identity that emphasized
equality of cultural attainments over differences of official
rank. Yet such equality did not extend to that lower fringe
of the elite, the first-degree holders, who had not yet (in

Wei Yuan's description of himself) "achieved eligibility for office."[4]

Literati participation, Wei implied, was one remedy for the ills of his own day. If brought to reality, it would fortify the political system against the kind of narrow-based factional tyranny exemplified by Heshen. It would mobilize a broader response to the economic and social chaos brought on by the currency crisis. And he certainly believed that it would contribute to the legitimacy and longevity of dynastic power. Nevertheless, we search Wei's writings in vain for any institutions through which literati participation might be exercised.

The style of Wei and his colleagues was to concentrate on practical issues, and beginning in the 1820s, no issue seemed more urgent a target, or more promising a political arena, than the Grain Transport Administration (*caoyun*). This huge, creaky, and costly sector of the bureaucracy had wreaked widespread destruction upon the provincial administration of central China. Wei Yuan estimated that the costs of the system had been out of hand for more than a century (which would place the origins of the trouble late in the Kangxi reign). Its destructive effects had long been visible in the provinces, but only gave rise to a major reform campaign in the 1820s, when the currency crisis was raising the price of every administrative abuse. The rapidly escalating cost of collecting and transporting Beijing's grain supply from the Yangzi valley was due as much to the greed of commercialized tax collectors as to the deterioration of the Grand Canal. Wei Yuan lamented that, "above, the people are paying millions in grain to serve public needs; while

[4]WYJ, p. 398.

below, they are paying millions in transport expenses to feed private demands."[5]

These "demands" came from layer upon layer of middlemen who lived off the system. No issue could have been better calculated to enlist broad support within the provincial bureaucracy: not only were official careers blighted by failure to meet tax quotas, but taxpayer anger was eroding official control over the countryside. We considered, in the preceding chapter, what it led to in Leiyang and other counties where the Grain Transport surtaxes ignited armed revolt. Wei Yuan knew that the threat to small landowners was at the same time a mortal threat to the regime; any state greedy enough to ruin the independent farmers would be digging its own grave: "Grieving that their land would be lost, and that they would become landless again, they would no longer submit to official control. What a disaster!"[6] Quoting *The Book of Odes*, Wei warned of the farmers' reaction to such a regime: "Never have you cared for my welfare. I shall leave you and journey to that fortunate land."[7]

By the 1850s, however, the system was no better. While the Taiping Rebellion was at its height, Feng Guifen reported that the Grain Transport taxes in Jiangnan were tearing society apart. Farmers were meeting tax collectors with violence. "Now at last," he wrote (quoting Mencius), "the people have paid back the conduct of their officers toward them."[8]

For the reformers of the 1820s, the short-term answer

[5]WYJ, pp. 413–16.
[6]WYJ, p. 73.
[7]WYJ, p. 72. Couvreur, p. 119.
[8]Feng Guifen, *Xianzhitang ji* 5:33. The passage from Mencius appears in the context of a popular uprising in which officials have been killed. Legge, *Mencius*, p. 173.

was to bypass the costly Grand Canal transport system and allow merchants to ship Yangzi grain to Beijing by sea. Once sea transport had defused the explosive countryside, Wei Yuan believed, "the people and the officials will cherish each other like kinsmen."[9] The provincial reformers were able to persuade the court to override the entrenched interests of the Grain Transport Administration and to ship rice by sea for the year 1826, but the experiment was abandoned the following year.[10]

The campaign for sea transport reveals the limits of 1820s reformism. Wei Yuan's solution was not to transform local administration but to relieve the small farmers of financial distress. Sea transport would lighten the most immediate burdens of the villages without addressing the constitutional problems of local society. His younger colleague Feng Guifen, however, who had fled his home before the Taiping rebel armies and had witnessed the humiliating "Second Opium War," was radicalized more decisively. His remedy for rural ills was accordingly more drastic: a finer network of political control in village society.

As a rallying point for reform, Grain Transport was suddenly overtaken in the 1830s by the crisis on the coast. The opium question and the ensuing war with Britain inflamed Chinese politics; the relatively undogmatic reformism of the 1820s gave way to moralistic denunciations of entrenched

[9]WYJ, p. 405.
[10]Not until 1847 was it undertaken again, once the throne had realized that grain collection was being seriously compromised by the expenses of Grand Canal shipment. Wei Hsiu-mei, *Tao Shu zai Jiangnan* (Taipei: Academia Sinica, 1985), pp. 102–18. Lin Man-houng, "Ziyou fangren jingji sixiang zai shijiu shiji chuye Zhongguodi ang'yang," *Zhongguo lishi xuehui shixue jikan* 25 (1993), pp. 127–28. Jane Kate Leonard, *Controlling From Afar: The Daoguang Emperor's Management of the Grand Canal Crisis, 1824–1826* (Ann Arbor, Mich.: Center for Chinese Studies, University of Michigan, 1996).

powerholders. The literati faction that pressed for an uncompromising anti-opium policy included some real outsiders (such as Wei Yuan's friend Gong Zizhen). From the late 1830s, the policy of militant resistance to the West became identified with activism by literati, many of whom were of low official rank or actually outside government.[11]

Wei Yuan had been involved in all the stages of reformist politics since the 1820s, and his younger contemporary, Feng Guifen, from the 1830s. To discover how these men understood what they were doing, however, we must discard any conception of a separate "literati interest" as such, any sense of an inevitable confrontation between literati and powerholders. Literati were no "third estate," long repressed by an arrogant aristocracy and seeking their historic destiny according to some general conception of rights or some long-range trend of history. As Wei Yuan and Feng Guifen perceived it, the job at hand was to fortify the political system that nourished their culture and ensured their status. Yet if that system were to survive, it had to adapt to the unprecedented conditions of the age.

Repeated humiliation by foreigners after the 1840s generated a new atmosphere of political rancor and new opportunities for attacking the policies of men in power. Those attacks assumed the moralistic, confrontational style known as "principled criticism" (*qingyi*), and its practitioners, the militants of the 1870s and 1880s, were known as the "principled (lit. pure) party" (*qingliu*). This loosely affiliated group of officials denounced men in power (particularly Li Hongzhang, who had to seek terms from the French) for their appeasement of foreign powers. The nasty innuendo

[11]James Polachek, *The Inner Opium War.*

was that appeasement stemmed from disloyalty and self-interest. But compared to Wei Yuan's conception of literati participation, "principled criticism" rested on rather narrow constitutional grounds. Indeed, it flourished at a time when some reform-minded officials considered that *too many* low-ranking men had wormed their way into government posts. A leader of the "principled criticism" group, Zhang Peilun, was alarmed by the hordes of low-status upstarts frantically pursuing government office:

Once the rank-purchase system was instituted on a large scale, a clamorous restlessness arose among the scholars, farmers, and merchants. The evil results have been confusion among social distinctions, and a disruption of the proper relationship between public and private. If everyone in the kingdom has exalted rank, then there can be no proper order.[12]

The official effort to rebuild the established order, following the destructive Taiping rebellion, included numerous proposals to purify the bureaucracy by narrowing its ports of entry: to limit the access of the new men from military and commercial backgrounds, who had begun to move into official posts through military merit or through outright purchase. The socially conservative atmosphere in which *qingyi* arose was reflected in its narrow social base: it was entirely confined to the bureaucracy itself. Its proponents did not attempt to mobilize support from among the broader group of literati, but sought to enhance their own image, and their own prospects, within the bureaucratic establishment. Far

---

[12]Wang Xianqian, *Guangxu chao donghualu* (Shanghai: 1909; reprint Beijing: Zhonghua shuju, 1984), p. 1473, memorial by Zhang Peilun, 1883. See also Chen Yongqin, "Wan-Qing qingliupai sixiang yanjiu," *Jindaishi yanjiu* (1993.3), p. 47.

less did they advance any argument from principle, that established literati as a group should be granted the privilege of criticizing the conduct of high officials, much less a wider public. Yet by linking the issue of wider participation to the issue of national defense, the "principled criticism" group palpably raised the political temperature of the age.

Indeed, the realities of life after 1860 were running counter to conservative constitutional thinking. Local elites (not all of them "established literati" by any means) had already achieved control over such lucrative new institutions as the commercial tax known as *likin*. In both rural and urban areas, the rebuilding of local society was being managed by established literati and by lower-status men as well: education, poor relief, and local security were urgent local tasks that the regular bureaucracy had to delegate to community notables, to an extent unknown a century earlier. And in great commercial cities such as Hankow in the central Yangzi valley, merchant guilds were assuming a more prominent role, under official patronage, in the administration of local services.

Therefore it is not surprising that, twenty years later, when literati participation was forcefully asserted as a principle, it was already being superseded in practice by broader formats of political action. The constitutional turning point was the spring of 1895, as the elite reacted furiously against the humiliating peace treaty just concluded with Japan. On the surface, it seemed as if the principle of literati participation was about to be realized. Literati reaction took the form, constitutionally speaking, of "petitions," submitted through the Censorate, by candidates for the highest (metropolitan) examination. These men were not in any sense "students," but *juren*, provincial degree-holders of the *de facto* national elite, and the kind of established literati that Wei Yuan had in mind as legitimate participants in national affairs. The sight of hundreds of such men, from sixteen provinces, voicing their outrage at the gates of government offices in Beijing would have left him astonished but delighted.

But the actual content of the "ten-thousand-word letter" drafted by Kang Youwei and signed by some 1,200 provincial-degree holders, went much further than Wei Yuan could have foreseen. The general populace was to elect representatives ("without regard to whether or not they have held government office") to serve in Beijing as "Court Gentlemen for Consultation" (*yilang*, a Han-dynasty term), who would offer criticism of imperial commands and serve as spokesmen for the people.

Above, they are to broaden His Majesty's sagelike understanding, so that he can sit in one hall and know the four seas. Below, they are to bring together the minds and wills of the empire, so that all can share cares and pleasures, forgetting the distinction between public and private . . . Sovereign and people will be of one body, and China will be as one family . . . So when funds are to be raised, what sums cannot be raised? When soldiers are to be trained, what numbers cannot be trained? With 400 million minds as one mind: how could the empire be stronger?[13]

Here we are already in the conceptual world of the modern nation-state as mediated by the Meiji Constitution in Japan. Such ideas were only conceivable under the duress of imminent foreign conquest, or even (in the social-Darwinian vocabulary of 1890s imperialism) of racial extinction.

[13]Zhongguo shixue hui, ed., *Zhong-Ri zhanzheng* (Beijing, 1961), vol. 2, p.153. For a study and a translation of this manifesto, see Kang Youwei, *Manifeste à l'empereur adressé par les candidats au doctorat*, translated, annotated, and presented by Roger Darrobers (Paris: You-feng, 1996).

Particularly striking in this vision of the nation is its leveling effect. Nationhood is the common property of all Chinese, of high station or low. The concept is similar in structure to the old idea that literati, whether in office or not, were equal in their common cultural status. But membership in the nation was, if anything, the more significant, because it was ascribed naturally by birth, rather than achieved through government. In practical terms, Kang Youwei's lieutenants were reaching beyond the "established literati" to mobilize the cultural elite at large through the "study societies" (*xuehui*) of the late 1890s, which were really centers for radical propaganda. Although provincial literati were their immediate targets, their publications reached a much wider audience, and their implied message was that the nation was not merely a literati concern.

Most inflammatory, however, was the idea that foreign conquest was linked to domestic tyranny. By the turn of the century, this view was evidently widespread. Consider these passages by a revolutionary and a constitutional monarchist, both written in 1903. Thus wrote Zou Rong: "[Evil rulers] arrogated to themselves titles of king and emperor, so that in the end nobody in the empire could enjoy equality or freedom. So, Genghiz Khan . . . and others, nomads of inferior stock, could enter China and make themselves master."[14] And thus Liang Qichao:

Powerful men of the same race can seize dictatorial power, and the nation will have to obey them. Violent and lawless foreigners can seize control, and the nation will have to obey them . . . Our people (*guomin*) have been governed by others for several thou-

[14]Zou Rong, *The Revolutionary Army*, trans. John Lust (The Hague: Mouton, 1968), p. 101.

sand years, and by now almost consider that to submit is their natural duty.[15]

"Governed by others," as Liang saw it, meant government by any power, foreign or domestic, that did not rest upon the universal participation of the people. Although the concept of participation by established literati may have played some transitional role in the minds of Liang Qichao and his colleagues, it was clearly inadequate to meet the emergency of the late 1890s. Presumably Liang and his followers saw that concept as too heavily mortgaged to state power, too socially exclusive to be generalized to the mass of the population. It conveyed no implications for social leveling, no concept of universal citizenship. In the event, however, Liang's view of participation was not based on individual rights, but upon the natural duty of all citizens to their community.

By the early years of the twentieth century, ideas of participation were being expressed in China through a special conception of community that was drawn from practical experience. I have mentioned how the reestablishment of order after the Taiping Rebellion drew nonofficial elites into public life, in cities and townships throughout China.[16] The "new policies" (*xinzheng*) of the Qing court after 1901,

[15]Liang Qichao, "Lun zizhi," *Yinbingshi heji* (Shanghai, 1941). *Zhuanji*, vol. 3, p. 54. *Guomin*, as used here by Liang, renders the Japanese *kokumin*, which conveys the Western idea of "a people within a nation state, a citizenry."

[16]The leading studies are Mary B. Rankin, *Elite Activism and Political Transformation in China: Zhejiang Province, 1865–1911* (Stanford, Calif.: Stanford University Press, 1986); and William T. Rowe, *Hankow: Commerce and Society in a Chinese City, 1796–1889* (Stanford, Calif.: Stanford University Press, 1985), and the second volume, *Hankow: Conflict and Community in a Chinese City, 1796–1895* (Stanford, Calif.: Stanford University Press, 1989).

however, were a more powerful engine of transformation. Here was a net gain of power and wealth: opportunities for local modernization (modern-style schools, street lighting, police, poor relief) that offered power and status outside the official system. The "new policies" offered local elites an opportunity to address the old problem of finding a revenue base for community needs, one beyond the reach of corrupt local governments. This might have seemed to them, if they could have so expressed it, the end of the old zero-sum game in Chinese local politics: the development of a modern nation offered an ever-expanding realm of power within which new groups could compete.

Without offering further detail on a well-studied subject, however, let us consider here only its constitutional meaning. Bringing merchants and lower elite, graduates of new-style schools and students returned from abroad into public life was a hallmark of the new community. Old barriers to political participation were falling. Equally striking was the idea that local self-government (*zizhi*) was not a gift of the central state, nor did it depend upon institutions run from Beijing. Energies from below, which had been patronized grudgingly by the old regime to combat its mortal enemies during the rebellions, now seemed fully legitimate as China prepared for constitutional government.

Apportioning power and reconciling interests are the essence of constitutionalism; a constitutional agenda faces up to the inevitability of social conflict and seeks ways of dealing with it. Chinese public life in the modern age would surely embody the unresolved agenda items of the Old Regime: the relationships between broader participation and autocratic rule, between political competition and the general good, and between local communities and the demands of the central state. In these respects, it is astonishing how poorly Chinese self-government proponents faced up to the realities of their age. The most eloquent and influential among them, Liang Qichao, considered that these old contradictions would dissolve under the liberating force of community self-government. He proposed that self-discipline (the mental component of self-government) would serve as the internal gyroscope of every citizen and every group; and that compulsion from an external bureaucracy would therefore be needless. The rules of social behavior, he wrote, "are not forged by some outside power, or by the emergence of one man. They stem from the common social conscience (*liangxin*). [Therefore] . . . they do not depend upon compulsion or force." Such internalized social discipline is the essence of self-government, he wrote. In its extreme form,

A man is like a machine; he himself decides how to prepare, initiate, and carry out his life's aims. . . . If an individual can behave this way, and if everyone else can, then the group can be self-governing . . . [The self-governing group] is like an army. Advancing together, stopping together. . . . Nobody fails to observe the public rules, nobody fails to seek the group's advantage. Men like this, and groups like this . . . [must certainly] stand strong in the world.

To anyone who objects to the images of machines and armies, Liang replies that "What a commander is to an army, the rules formed by everyone's social conscience are to a group." This cannot be called autocracy (*zhuan*), "because the rules come from the multitude and not from one man."[17]

[17]Liang, "Lun zizhi," *Yinbingshi heji, zhuanji*, vol. 3, p. 52.

We are offered, here, a magic even stronger than "the invisible hand," because the existence of community conflict is not even acknowledged. For the word "group" Liang uses the old term *qun*, which, with the ancient meaning of "sociability," we have already observed in Wei Yuan's writings. To the reformist of the 1830s, as to the nationalist of the 1900s, the term meant political activism without taint of faction. Obviously neither Wei nor Liang was so unworldly as to ignore the natural clash of opinions and private interests in politics. The point is rather that both men evidently considered it important to ward off criticism grounded on imputation of factional motives. In Wei's case, the long background of dynastic hostility to factions forced him to tread carefully. For Liang, the imperative of national unity must have enhanced the attractiveness of the bland expression *qun*, with its connotations of disinterested activism and group solidarity. He had to persuade his readers that more energetic political involvement need not provoke internal disunity.

It is characteristic of Liang's writing, in this period, to insist that the essence of constitutionalism lay not in its mechanics (elections and assemblies) but in its spirit. The seemingly inevitable conflicts are dissolved by giving free reign to man's natural social feelings, particularly those of the local community. "Western political writers say that nothing is more important than the small kingdoms within a nation. These small kingdoms are a province, a prefecture, a department, a county, a township, a city, a commercial corporation, a school. Each of these has exactly the form of a nation."[18] Yet between these self-governing "small king-

[18]Ibid., p. 54.

doms" and the larger national unit, there is no conflict. The nation is simply an "enlarged picture" of the small kingdoms, so that if these kingdoms can be "self-governing," then the nation can simply follow suit by putting national self-government into effect. Characteristic, too, is Liang's focus on national power. His cynosure was the world's most powerful industrial and imperialist state. Britain ruled half the world "because the Anglo-Saxon race is the one most abundantly provided with self-governing power."[19]

About Western political systems, Liang was certainly one of the best informed of his generation. Yet the lens through which he viewed them revealed to him the *results* of the British political system (that is to say, national power) more clearly than it did its *historical origins*. A further distortion arose from the vocabulary in which Liang expressed the idea of self-government. The imported idea of "self-government" seemed to resemble an old complex of Chinese ideas about "feudal monarchy" (*fengjian*), a style of political argumentation based upon an alternative vision of human nature. In this vision, compulsion by centrally appointed bureaucrats could never produce as benign a government as could empowerment of local leaders to run their own communities. And this principle was pronounced to be consistent with a unified China and a long-lasting dynasty.[20]

This vision had been conceived by Old Regime critics of autocratic central power; could it be transformed to serve the modern state? Was the modern state really to be achieved through such effortless conformity between local

[19]Ibid., p. 51.
[20]Min Tu-ki, "The Theory of Political Feudalism in the Ch'ing Period," *National Polity and Local Power: The Transformation of Late Imperial China* (Cambridge, Mass.: Harvard University, Council on East Asian Studies, 1989), pp. 89–136.

and national interests? Although the idea of building national power from the bottom up continued to be influential in twentieth-century constitutional thought, including that of Sun Yatsen (1866–1925), it quickly got a cold shower of skepticism from the revolutionary leader Zhang Binglin (1869–1936).

In his critique of representative government, Zhang attacked the "feudal monarchy" vision in terms rather like those expressed by Feng Guifen's critics in 1898. The way to build a strong state, he insisted, was not to entrust power to local people, but to reform the regular bureaucracy. In present circumstances, local self-government would open the way to widespread concealment of taxable land, obviously not what was needed by a powerful unified nation. Only when bureaucrats were ruthlessly punished for corruption would the people support their government. Only when the people could see their taxes being used for public good rather than private gain, would they willingly pay them.[21] England and Japan, the countries whose "self-government" was admired in China, were historically just a step away from feudalism, Zhang pointed out, while China was two millennia removed from her feudal age. China was indeed the type of society best suited to centralized bureaucratic control. Its underlying egalitarianism, its lack of hereditary estates and castes, made possible an equal application of the laws by central authority. This social equality was a precious asset; Europe and America, where wealth and privilege ruled politics, could not match it. In China, community self-government would only spawn a new breed of local

[21]Zhang Binglin, "Zhengwen sheyuan dahui pohuai zhuang," *Minbao* 17 (25 Oct. 1907), pp. 1–7.

elites who would clamp their own tyranny upon the villages. Instead, China's course must be equal application of the laws and rigorous discipline of the bureaucracy.[22] Was there a certain mysticism in the views of both men? Liang's faith that national strength and unity would emerge naturally from self-governing communities required a human nature cleansed of greed and ambition. If self-interested social elites were to define the interest of the community, what benefit would accrue to the nation? Yet the threat to China's survival in a Darwinian world seemed to require nothing less than a self-regulating citizenry, which would make unnecessary a self-serving bureaucracy. Self-government seemed the only possible counterpoise to despotism — which, in Liang's view, fostered the political lassitude that could lead only to foreign conquest and racial extinction.

In the light of China's twentieth-century experience, Zhang Binglin's views seem equally mystical. To expect state agencies to treat citizens with fairness and restraint, without some countervailing community strength to insist upon it, seems an invitation to despotism. Yet his vision of a disciplined bureaucracy's offering impartial justice and protecting common citizens from the elites of their own communities was an appealing one in the context of late imperial society.

Two voices in the tumultuous last decade of empire, Liang and Zhang offer a negative paradigm of events to come. China's twentieth-century history has dashed the

[22]Zhang Binglin, "Daiyi ranfou lun," *Minbao* 24 (10 Oct. 1908), 1–27. Also see Zhang, "Dongjing liuxuesheng huanying hui yanshuo ci," (1906), Tang Zhijun, ed., *Zhang Taiyan zhenglun xuanji* (Beijing: Zhonghua shuju, 1977), 277–78; Chang Hao, *Chinese Intellectuals in Crisis: The Search for Order and Meaning, 1890–1911* (Berkeley: University of California Press, 1987), pp. 104–45.

hopes of both. Liang's vision of a self-governing constitutional state offered no counterweight to militarized despotisms, whether provincial or national; while Zhang's vision of a closely regulated bureaucracy, dispensing equal justice to equal citizens, foundered on the old difficulty of placing government under law. As Liang Qichao pointed out (describing the Qing dynasty), "China has laws, but the officials themselves do not obey them, to say nothing of the common people."[23]

From year to year, the story of twentieth-century politics is chaotic and multidirectional. Viewed over a century, it is a story about the relentless march of the central state. The monarchy's immediate successors did their best to replace the "self-government" bodies of the 1910s with centers of bureaucratic administration. Provincial regimes (such as that of Yan Xishan in Shanxi) experimented with new kinds of state agents on the village level. And although the Guomindang assumed power in 1927 committed to Sun Yatsen's program of self-government from the ground up, it too set about bureaucratizing local society by drawing new administrative divisions below the county and by stripping local communities of even their nominal self-governing functions. At length, the authoritarian side of the Sun Yatsen legacy triumphed decisively over the communitarian side. In the cities, the birth-cries of "civil society" were cut short. Commercial, professional, and civic associations, labor and student unions, were brought increasingly under state control by the Guomindang regime, until after 1949, the People's Republic either destroyed them or bent them into tools of state regulation.

[23]Liang, "Lun zizhi," p. 52.

The Communist revolutionary program envisaged a strong, industrialized nation. In retrospect, it was logical that the Party link the rhetoric of community and participation to the needs of the state. During the war against Japan, for example, rural elections were subtly transformed into vehicles for state control: representatives to township assemblies would serve as local agents of the township bureaucrats when the assemblies were not in session.[24] Such transformations were made easier by the old ambiguity of the Chinese term for "self-government": it could mean either local communities running their own affairs, or administering that community (collecting taxes, enforcing laws) on behalf of state authorities. But the final blows to communitarian ideas were land reform and collectivization. Class labels cut communities apart, and collective property became a tool for the state to run a more efficient system of rural taxation. To achieve control of grain for the nourishment of the cities, the state destroyed the old rural market communities and turned the market towns into centers of government administration. It is hard to escape the conclusion that early twentieth-century theories of universal participation were grandly designed but weakly structured; whereas state-building by twentieth-century governments was able to draw upon the deep administrative experience of the Old Regime.

Since the Maoist era ended and China entered the "reform era," the modern constitutional agenda has again become subject to lively debate. It still includes the old problems of defining the boundaries of participation, of defining an acceptable relationship between public interest and pri-

[24]Chen Yung-fa, *Making Revolution: The Communist Movement in Eastern and Central China, 1937–1945* (Berkeley: University of California Press, 1986), p. 226.

vate interests, of reconciling the needs of the central state
with those of local communities. To resolve these problems
in late imperial times was difficult enough. Whether they
can be resolved in a regionally diverse national unit of more
than a billion people cannot be foreseen, because such a national unit has never before existed in human history.

That China entered her modern age as a unified nation
seems such an obvious fact that its significance has largely
escaped us. Despite widespread talk of the "breakup of
China," or its being "carved up" by foreign powers, both
the fact and the idea of central government in a single Chinese state survived the terrible years of warlordism, foreign
invasion, and civil war. Throughout the early experiments
with local self-government, political activists in provinces
and municipalities represented their actions in terms of national salvation. Even during the chaotic warlord years, no
provincial separatism, and no federalist proposal, could
stand against the overwhelming attraction of national unity
among the Chinese people.[25] Unity, with its practical re-
quirement of centralized leadership, has placed extraordinary demands upon China's constitutional agenda.

Historically, Chinese unity has been imposed by military
force, and behind the civilianized regimes that followed the
conquerors, military force has stood not far offstage. A national elite without hereditary status looked to the central
regime to certify its local preeminence with academic degrees and to replenish its wealth through official employment. Ideological conformity, which was the conqueror's
to impose, was the price for those benefits. Although that

[25]Prasenjit Duara, "Deconstructing the Chinese Nation," *The Australian Journal of Chinese Affairs* 30 (July 1993), pp. 1–26.

was a price not paid willingly by everyone, there were always more than enough conformers to maintain the system.

By the first decade of the twentieth century, it was generally accepted, in all political camps, that the central state must build up its military and economic strength on behalf of the nation's "wealth and power." Despite much disagreement as to who ought to control that state, the aim of state-building was not seriously questioned. For this consensus was exacted a heavy price in intellectual subservience and political manipulation. Most disappointing to Chinese intellectuals, perhaps, has been the continuing force of the old objection to political competition. If there is a single public interest, then surely self-interested competition among political groups must undermine it. The absorption of this old idea by absolutist political parties has an unhappily familiar ring to Chinese intellectuals.

One cannot assume, however, that national unity has the same constitutional force in present-day China as it did in earlier times. The post-Mao opening to world commerce may have opened the door to *de facto* self-government in the coastal provinces, at least in economic affairs.[26] Old ideas about participation, public interest, and local community may in time be redefined in ways that have less to do with the centralized state. It remains to be seen whether a modern Chinese state can be designed without reference to a narrowly based, doctrinaire central authority. Many Chinese now think it can. If so, however, we can expect that the Chinese constitutional agenda will still be addressed on China's terms, not on ours.

[26]Philip A. Kuhn, "Can China Be Governed From Beijing? Reflections on Reform and Regionalism," in Wang Gungwu and John Wong, eds., *China's Political Economy* (Singapore: Singapore University Press, 1998), pp. 149–66.

REFERENCE MATTER

Bibliography

Ash, Robert. "The Evolution of Agricultural Policy," *China Quarterly* 116 (Dec. 1988), pp. 529–55.

Bartlett, Beatrice S. *Monarchs and Ministers: The Grand Council in Mid-Ch'ing China, 1723–1820*. Berkeley: University of California Press, 1991.

Bernstein, Thomas P. "Stalinism, Famine, and Chinese Peasants: Grain Procurements During the Great Leap Forward," *Theory and Society* 13:3 (1984), pp. 339–77.

Bo Yibo 薄一波. *Ruogan zhongda juece yu shijian de huigu* 若干重大決策與實踐的回顧 (Memoirs of some important decisions and events). Beijing: Zhonggong zhongyang dangxiao chubanshe, 1991.

Bosher, John Francis. *French Finances 1770–1795: From Business to Bureaucracy*. Cambridge, Eng.: Cambridge University Press, 1970.

Chang, Hao. *Chinese Intellectuals in Crisis: The Search for Order and Meaning, 1890–1911*. Berkeley: University of California Press, 1987.

Chen Ding 陳鼎. "Jiaobinlu kangyi bielun" 校邠盧抗議別論 (A separate discussion of the *Jiaobinlu kangyi*). Manuscript held at First Historical Archives, Beijing.

Chen Yaonan (Chan Yiu-nam) 陳耀南. *Wei Yuan yanjiu* 魏源研究 (A study of Wei Yuan). Hong Kong: Zhaoming chubanshe, 1979.

Chen Yaonan 陳耀南, Li Hanwu 李漢武, and Tang Zhijun 湯志鈞. "Wei Yuan de bianyi sixiang he Shi, Shu guwei" 魏源的變易思想和

詩書古微 (Wei Yuan's reformist thinking and the "Ancient subtleties of the Odes and Documents"). In Yang Shenzhi 楊慎之 and Huang Liyong 黃麗鏞, eds., *Wei Yuan sixiang yanjiu* 魏源思想研究 (Studies on Wei Yuan's thought). Changsha: Hunan renmin chubanshe, 1987, pp. 170–90.

Chen Yongqin 陳永勤. "Wan-Qing qingliupai sixiang yanjiu" 晚清清流派思想研究 (The thought of the late Qing pure clique). *Jindaishi yanjiu* 75:3 (1993), pp. 44–61.

Chen Yung-fa. *Making Revolution: The Communist Movement in Eastern and Central China, 1937–1945.* Berkeley: University of California Press, 1986.

Church, Clive. "The Process of Bureaucratization in France, 1789–1799." In *Die Französische Revolution—zufälliges oder notwendiges Ereignis?* Munich: Oldenbourg Verlag GmbH., 1983, vol. 1, pp. 121–37.

Couvreur, Séraphin, S.J. *Cheu King.* 3d ed. Sien-hien: Imprimerie de la Mission Catholique, 1934.

Crossley, Pamela Kyle. *Orphan Warriors: Three Manchu Generations and the End of the Qing World.* Princeton, N.J.: Princeton University Press, 1990.

Da Qing huidian shili 大清會典事例 (Statutes and precedents of the Qing dynasty). Guangxu edition, 1898; reprint, Taipei: Zhongwen shuju, 1963.

Ding Weizhi 丁偉志. "Jiaobinlu kangyi yu Zhongguo wenhua jindaihua" 校邠盧抗議與中國文化近代化 (The *Jiaobinlu kangyi* and the modernization of Chinese culture). *Lishi yanjiu* 5 (1993), pp. 74–91.

Duara, Prasenjit. *Culture, Power, and the State: Rural North China, 1900–1942.* Stanford, Calif.: Stanford University Press, 1988.

Dunstan, Helen. "The 'Autocratic Heritage' and China's Political Future: A View from a Qing Specialist," *Eastern Asian History* 12 (1996), pp. 79–104.

Elman, Benjamin. *Classicism, Politics, and Kinship: The Ch'ang-chou School of New Text Confucianism in Late Imperial China.* Berkeley: University of California Press, 1990.

———. *A Cultural History of Civil Examinations in Late Imperial China.* Berkeley: University of California Press, 2000.

Fei Hsiao-t'ung (Fei Xiaotong). *Peasant Life in China: A Field Study of Country Life in the Yangtze Valley.* New York: E. P. Dutton, 1939.

Feng Guifen 馮桂芬. *Xianzhitang ji* 顯志堂集 (Collected writings from the studio of illumining the will). Jiaobinlu ed., 1876; reprint Taipei: Xuehai chubanshe, 1981.

Feng Guifen 馮桂芬, *Jiaobinlu kangyi* 校邠盧抗議 (Essays of protest from the cottage where one studies the ancient system of the Zhou). 1897 edition; repr. Taipei, Xuehai chubanshe, 1967.

Feng Zuozhe 馮佐哲. *Heshen pingzhuan* 和珅評傳 (A critical biography of Heshen). Beijing: Zhongguo qingnian chubanshe, 1998.

Fischer, Wolfram, and Peter Lundgreen. "The Recruitment and Training of Administrative and Technical Personnel." In Charles Tilly, ed., *The Formation of National States in Western Europe*. Princeton, N.J.: Princeton University Press, 1975. pp. 456–61.

Gao Xiang 高翔. *Kang-Yong-Qian sandi tongzhi sixiang yanjiu* 康雍乾三帝統治思想研究 (The philosophies of governance of the Kangxi, Yongzheng, and Qianlong emperors). Beijing: Zhongguo renmin daxue chubanshe, 1995.

Gibbons, Michael T. "The Public Sphere, Commercial Society, and The Federalist Papers." In Wilson Carey McWilliams and Michael T. Gibbons, eds., *The Federalists, the Antifederalists, and the American Political Tradition*. Westport, Conn.: Greenwood Press, 1992, pp. 107–26.

Gu Yanwu 顧炎武. *Yuanchaoben Rizhilu* 原鈔本日知錄 (Record of daily knowledge, original manuscript version). Taipei: Minglun chubanshe, 1970.

Gunn, J. A. W. "Public Interest." In Terence Ball et al., eds., *Political Innovation and Conceptual Change*. Cambridge, Eng.: Cambridge University Press, 1989. pp. 194–210.

Guo Runtao 郭潤濤. "Changsui xingzheng shulun" 長隨行政述論 (The administrative work of private retainers of officials). *Qingshi yanjiu* 4 (1992), pp. 29–39.

Hamilton, Alexander, et al., *The Federalist, or The New Constitution: Papers by Alexander Hamilton, James Madison, and John Jay*. New York: Modern Library, 1941.

He Changling 賀長齡, ed. *Huangchao jingshi wenbian* 皇朝經世文編 (Collected essays on statecraft from the reigning dynasty). 1827 ed., reprint Shanghai: Hongwen'ge, 1898.

He Guangru 賀廣如. *Wei Moshen sixiang tanjiu—yi chuantong jingdian de quanshuo wei taolun zhongxin* 魏默深思想探究—以傳統經典的詮說爲討論中心 (A study of Wei Yuan's thought, based on explication of the classics). Taibei: Guoli Taiwan daxue, 1999.

Hightower, James R. *Han Shih Wai Chuan: Han Ying's Illustration of the Didactic Application of the Classic of Songs.* Cambridge, Mass.: Harvard University Press, 1952.

Ho, Ping-ti. *Studies on the Population of China.* Cambridge, Mass.: Harvard University Press, 1959.

Huang Liyong 黃麗鏞. *Wei Yuan nianpu* 魏源年譜 (Chronological biography of Wei Yuan). Changsha: Hunan renmin chubanshe, 1985.

Huangchao wenxian tongkao 皇朝文獻通考 (Documentary encyclopedia of the Qing dynasty). Taipei: Qianlong ed., reprint Taipei: Geda shuju, 1963.

Jin Guantao 金觀濤 and Liu Qingfeng 劉青峰. "Zhongguo Gongchandang weishenme fangqi xinminzhu zhuyi?" 中國共產黨為什麼放棄新民主主義 (Why did the Chinese Communist Party abandon New Democracy?) *Ershiyi shiji shuangyue kan* (Oct. 1992), pp. 13–25.

Jones, Susan Mann. "Hung Liang-chi (1746–1809): The Perception and Articulation of Political Problems in Late Eighteenth-Century China." Ph.D. diss., Stanford University, 1972.

Kang Youwei. *Manifeste à l'Empereur Adressé Par les Candidats au Doctorat.* Trans. and annotated by Roger Darrobers. Paris: You-feng, 1996.

Kuhn, Philip A. "Late Ch'ing Views of the Polity." In *Select Papers from the Center for Far Eastern Studies,* University of Chicago, 4 (1979–1980), pp. 1–18.

———. "Can China be Governed From Beijing? Reflections on Reform and Regionalism." In Wang Gungwu and John Wong, eds., *China's Political Economy.* Singapore: Singapore University Press, 1988, pp. 149–66.

———. and John K. Fairbank. *Introduction to Ch'ing Documents: The Rebellion of Chung Jen-chieh.* Cambridge, Mass.: Harvard–Yenching Institute, 1993.

———. *Les Origines de l'État Chinois Moderne.* Traduit et présenté par Pierre-Étienne Will. Paris: Cahiers des Annales, distributed by Armand Colin, 1999.

Kupersmith, Abraham. "Montesquieu and the Ideological Strain in Antifederalist Thought." In Wilson Carey McWilliams and Michael T. Gibbons, eds., *The Federalists, the Antifederalists, and the American Political Tradition.* Westport, Conn.: Greenwood Press, 1992, pp. 47–75.

Kuribayashi Nobuo 栗林宣夫. *Rikōsei no kenkyū* 里甲制の研究 (Study of the *lijia* system). Tokyo: Bunri shoin, 1971.

Legge, James, trans. *The Four Books: Confucian Analects, The Great Learning, The Doctrine of the Mean, and The Works of Mencius*. Shanghai: Chinese Book Co., 1933; reprint New York: Paragon Book Reprint Corp., 1966.

Leiyang xianzhi 耒陽縣志 (Gazetteer of Leiyang county). 1886 ed.

Leonard, Jane Kate. *Wei Yuan and China's Rediscovery of the Maritime World*. Cambridge, Mass.: Council on East Asian Studies, Harvard University, 1984.

———. *Controlling From Afar: The Daoguang Emperor's Management of the Grand Canal Crisis, 1824–1826*. Ann Arbor, Mich.: Center for Chinese Studies, University of Michigan, 1996.

Li Borong 李柏榮. *Wei Yuan shiyou ji* 魏源師友記 (Wei Yuan's teachers and friends). Changsha: Yuelu shushe, 1983.

Li Hanwu 李漢武. *Wei Yuan zhuan* 魏源傳 (Biography of Wei Yuan). Changsha: Hunan daxue chubanshe, 1988.

Li Kan 李侃 and Gong Shuduo 龔書鐸. "Wuxu bianfa shiqi dui *Jiaobinlu kangyi* de yici pinglun—jieshao gugong bowuyuan Ming–Qing dang'anbu suocang Jiaobinlu kangyi qianzhuben" 戊戌變法時期對校邠盧抗議的一次評論—介紹故宮博物院明清檔案部所藏校邠盧抗議箋註本 (A critique of *Jiaobinlu kangyi* from the period of the 1898 Reform—introducing the comments on *Jiaobinlu kangyi* in the Ming-Qing archives of the Palace Museum).*Wenwu* 7 (1978), pp. 53–59.

Liang Qichao 梁啓超. *Yinbingshi heji, zhuanji* 飲冰室合集專集 (Collected works from the ice drinker's studio, specialized articles). Shanghai: Zhonghua shuju, 1941.

Lin Man-houng 林滿紅. "Ziyou fangren jingji sixiang zai shijiu shiji chuye Zhongguodi angyang" 自由放任經濟思想在十九世紀初葉中國的昂揚 (The rise of laisser-faire economic thought in early nineteenth-century China). *Zhongguo lishi xuehui shixue jikan*, 25 (1993) 121–41.

Liu Cuirong 劉翠溶. "Qingchu Shunzhi Kangxi nianjian jianmien fushui di guocheng" 清初順治康熙年間減免賦稅的過程 (The process of reducing taxes during the Shunzhi and Kangxi reigns of the early Qing). In Zhou Kangxie 周康爕 ed., *Zhongguo jin sanbainian jingjishi lunji* 中國近三百年經濟史論集 (Studies of Chinese economic history

during the past three centuries), 2 vols. Hong Kong: Chongwen shuju, 1972.

Liu Guangjing (Kwang-ching Liu) 劉廣京. "Shijiu shiji chuye Zhongguo zhishi fenzi—Bao Shichen yu Wei Yuan" 十九世紀初葉中國知
識分子—包世臣與魏源 (Chinese intellectuals of the early nineteenth
century—Bao Shichen and Wei Yuan). In *Zhongyang yanjiuyuan
guoji Hanxue huiyi lunwenji* (Collected papers of the International Si-
nological Conference, Academia Sinica). Taipei: Academia Sinica,
1981, pp. 995–1030.

Lufu zouzhe nongmin yundong 録副奏摺農民運動 (Duplicate copies of
palace memorials relating to peasant movements). First Historical
Archives of China, Beijing.

Lu Shiqiang (Lü Shih-ch'iang) 呂實強. "Feng Guifen de zhengzhi sixiang" 馮桂芬的政治思想 (Feng Guifen's political thought). In
Zhonghua wenhua fuxing yuekan 4:2 (1971) 5–12.

Madison, James. *The Papers of James Madison*. ed. William Hutchinson
et al. Chicago: University of Chicago Press, 1962–1991, 17 vols.: vol.
11 (1977).

Mathias, Peter, and Patrick O'Brien. "Taxation in Britain and France
1715–1810: A Comparison of the Social and Economic Incidence of
Taxes Collected for the Central Governments," *Journal of European
Economic History*, 5:3 (1976), pp. 601–50.

Min, Tu-ki. *National Polity and Local Power: The Transformation of Late
Imperial China*. Cambridge, Mass.: Council on East Asian Studies,
Harvard University, 1989.

Mote, Frederick W., and Denis Twitchett, eds. *The Cambridge History of
China, Vol. 7: The Ming Dynasty, 1368–1644, Part I*. Cambridge, Eng.:
Cambridge University Press, 1988.

Naquin, Susan. *Peking: Temples and City Life, 1400–1900*. Berkeley: University of California Press, 2000.

Nivison, David S. "Ho-shen and His Accusers: Ideology and Political
Behavior in the 18th Century." In D. S. Nivison and Arthur F.
Wright, eds., *Confucianism in Action*. Stanford, Calif.: Stanford Uni-
versity Press, 1959, pp. 209–43.

Nongye jitihua zhongyang wenjian huibian 農業集體化中央文件匯編
(Collected documents on agricultural collectivization). Beijing:
Zhongyang dangxiao, 1981, 2 vols.

Oi, Jean C. *State and Peasant in Contemporary China: The Political Economy of Village Government.* Berkeley: University of California Press, 1989.

Peterson, Paul. "Antifederalist Thought in Contemporary American Politics." In Josephine F. Pacheco, ed., *Antifederalism: The Legacy of George Mason.* Fairfax, Va.: George Mason University Press, 1992, pp. 111–32.

Polachek, James. "Gentry Hegemony: Soochow in the T'ung-chih Restoration." In Frederic Wakeman and Carolyn Grant, eds., *Conflict and Control in Late Imperial China.* Berkeley: University of California Press, 1975, pp. 211–56.

———. *The Inner Opium War.* Cambridge, Mass.: Council on East Asian Studies, Harvard University, 1992.

Qi Sihe 齊思和, "Wei Yuan yu wan Qing xuefeng" 魏源與晚清學風 (Wei Yuan and late Qing scholarship). *Yanjing xuebao* 39 (1950), pp. 177–226.

Qinding siku quanshu 欽定四庫全書 (Imperially authorized complete library of the four treasuries). Taipei: Taiwan shangwu yinshuguan, 1983.

Qing shigao 清史稿 (Draft history of the Qing dynasty). Beijing: Zhonghua shuju, 1977.

Rankin, Mary B. *Elite Activism and Political Transformation in China: Zhejiang Province, 1865–1911.* Stanford, Calif.: Stanford University Press, 1986.

Reed, Bradly W. *Talons and Teeth: County Clerks and Runners in the Qing Dynasty.* Stanford, Calif.: Stanford University Press, 2000.

Rowe, William T., "Hu Lin-i's Reform of the Grain Tribute System in Hupeh, 1855–1858," *Ch'ing-shih wen-t'i* 4:10 (December 1983), pp. 33–86.

———. *Hankow: Commerce and Society in a Chinese City, 1796–1889.* Stanford, Calif.: Stanford University Press, 1985.

———. *Hankow: Conflict and Community in a Chinese City, 1796–1895.* Stanford, Calif.: Stanford University Press, 1989.

———. *Saving the World: Chen Hongmou and Elite Consciousness in Eighteenth-Century China.* Stanford, Calif.: Stanford University Press, 2001.

Sazanami, Tomoko. "Fei Xiaotong's 1957 Critique of Agricultural Collectivization in a Chinese Village." In *Papers on Chinese History.* Cambridge, Mass.: The Fairbank Center, Harvard University, 2 (1993), pp. 19–32.

Shuilibu Huanghe shuili weiyuanhui 水利部黃河水利委員會 comp. *Huanghe shuilishi shuyao* 黃河水利史述要 (Essentials of the history of Yellow river conservancy). Beijing: Shuili chubanshe, 1982.

Skinner, G. William, ed. *The City in Late Imperial China*. Stanford, Calif.: Stanford University Press, 1977.

Stokes, Eric. *The English Utilitarians and India*. Oxford: Clarendon Press, 1959.

Tocqueville, Alexis de. *L'Ancien Régime et la Révolution*. Paris: Gallimard, 1967.

Van Zoeren, Steven Jay. *Poetry and Personality: Reading, Exegesis, and Hermeneutics in Traditional China*. Stanford, Calif.: Stanford University Press, 1991.

Wang Jiajian 王家儉. *Wei Yuan nianpu* 魏源年譜 (Chronological biography of Wei Yuan). Taipei: Jinghua shuju, 1967.

Wang Xianqian 王先謙. *Guangxu chao donghualu* 光緒朝東華錄 (Records from the Donghua Gate, Guangxu reign). Shanghai: 1909; reprint Beijing: Zhonghua shuju, 1984.

Wang, Yeh-chien. *Land Taxation in Imperial China, 1750–1911*. Cambridge, Mass.: Harvard University Press, 1973.

Wei Xiumei 魏秀梅. *Tao Shu zai Jiangnan* 陶澍在江南 (Governor Tao Shu in Jiangnan). Taipei: Academia Sinica, 1985.

Wei Yuan 魏源. *Wei Yuan ji* 魏源集 (Collected works of Wei Yuan). Beijing: Zhonghua shuju, 1976.

Will, Pierre-Étienne. "Entre Passé et Présent." In Philip A. Kuhn, *Les Origines de l'État Chinois Moderne*. Traduit et présenté par Pierre-Étienne Will. Paris: Armand Colin, 1999, pp. 11–68.

Xue Yunsheng 薛允升. *Duli cunyi* 讀例存疑 (Questions arising while reading the substatutes). Taipei: Chinese Materials Center, 1970, 5 vols.

Yamamoto Eishi 山本英史. "Shinkin ni yoru suiryō hōran to Shinchō kokka" 紳衿による稅糧包攬と清朝國家 (Proxy-remittance of taxes by the literati and the Qing state). *Tōyōshi kenkyū* 48:4 (March 1990), pp. 40–69.

———. "Yōsei shinkin kōryō shobun kō" 雍正紳衿抗糧處分考 (Punishment of literati tax resistance during the Yongzheng reign). *Chūgoku kindaishi kenkyū* 7 (July 1992), pp. 78–115.

Zelin, Madeleine. *The Magistrate's Tael: Rationalizing Fiscal Reform in Eighteenth-Century Ch'ing China*. Berkeley: University of California Press, 1984.

Zeng Guofan 曾國藩. *Zeng Wenzheng gong quanji* 曾文正公全集 (Complete works of Zeng Guofan). Taipei: Shijie shuju, 1965, 3 vols.

Zhang Binglin 章炳麟. "Dongjing liuxuesheng huanyinghui yanshuoci" 東京留學生歡迎會演說詞 (Speech at the welcoming meeting held by Chinese students in Japan). In Tang Zhijun 湯志鈞, ed., *Zhang Taiyan zhenglun xuanji* 章太炎政論選集 (Selected political writings of Zhang Binglin). Beijing: Zhonghua shuju, 1977, pp. 277–78.

———. "Ji Zhengwen sheyuan dahui pohuaizhuang" 記政聞社員大會破壞狀 (Record of the disruption of the meeting of the Zhengwenshe), *Minbao* 17 (25 Oct. 1907), pp. 1–7.

———. "Daiyi ranfou lun" 代議然否論 (Pros and cons of representative government), *Minbao* 24 (10 Oct. 1908), pp. 1–27.

Zhao Liewen 趙烈文. *Nengjingjushi riji* 能靜居士日記 (Diary of a scholar who is capable of repose). Taipei: Xuesheng shuju, 1964.

Zhongguo shixuehui 中國史學會, ed. *Zhong-Ri zhanzheng* 中日戰爭 (The Sino-Japanese war). Shanghai: Renmin chubanshe, 1961, 7 vols.: vol. 2.

Zhu Xi 朱熹. *Zhuzi yulei* 朱子語類 (Sayings of Master Zhu). Taipei: Huashi chubanshe, 1987.

Zhupi zouzhe nongmin yundong 硃批奏摺農民運動 (Vermilion-endorsed palace memorials relating to peasant movements). First Historical Archives of China, Beijing.

Zou Rong. *The Revolutionary Army*, trans. John Lust. Paris, The Hague: Mouton, 1968.

Character List

bachi 把持
bagongsheng 拔貢生
baolan 包攬
baoshou 包收
Bo Yibo 薄一波
caichen 才臣
caoyun 漕運
Chen Ding 陳鼎
chengfen 成分
chengyi 城邑
Ch'en Hsi-yuan (Chen Xiyuan)
　陳熙遠
Chen Hu 陳瑚
Chunqiu 春秋
dang 黨
diaojin liedong 刁衿劣董
diaosheng liejian 刁生劣監
dibao 地保
difangzhi 地方志
Donglin 東林
Dongtai 東臺
Duan Bacui 段拔萃

fengjian 封建
fuqiang 富強
Fu xiangzhi yi 復鄉制議
Fuxing gongguan 福星公館
Gaoyou 高郵
Gong chuzhi yi 公黜陟議
gonglun 公論
Gong Zizhen 龔自珍
guan 觀
guanhu 官戶
guiji 詭寄
Guweitang neiji 古微堂內集
guwen 古文
Gu Yanwu 顧炎武
Haiguo tuzhi 海國圖志
He Changling 賀長齡
hedi 和糴
hezuohua 合作化
Hong Liangji 洪亮吉
hua 化
huidian 會典
Hu Linyi 胡林翼

huzhuzu 互助組
jianshu 諫書
jiaoyang 教養
Jijiu pian 急就篇
jin 衿
jingkong 京控
jingshi 經世
jinwen 今文
jitihua 集體化
ju 局
ju 舉
Ju Deyuan 鞠德源
Junxian lun 郡縣論
junzi 君子
Kong Xiangji 孔祥吉
kongyan 空言
kuangju 匡居
Lai Qingjian 賴清鍵
Leiyang 耒陽
Liang Renwang 梁人望
liangxin 良心
lichai 里差
lijia 里甲
likin (lijin) 厘金
lingchi 凌遲
Lin Man-houng (Lin Manhong)
    林滿紅
lishu 里書
liyuan 吏員
lougui 陋規
Lu 魯
Lufei Quan 陸費瑔
lufu zouzhe 錄副奏摺
Luming 鹿鳴
Lunyu 論語
Lun zizhi 論自治
Luo Bingzhang 駱秉章
minfeng 民風

minqian 民欠
mo er shi zhi 默而識之
Mogu 默觚
mufu 幕府
muyou 幕友
Muzhang'a 穆彰阿
nengchen 能臣
pengdang 朋黨
Pengdang lun 朋黨論
Puqiu 溥丘
Qi 齊
qianzhi 牽制
qianzhu 簽註
qiaohuan 巧宦
qigu yu zhong yi 奇觚與眾異
qingliu 清流
qingyi 清議
qu 區
qun 群
qun er bu dang 群而不黨
shanxing 善行
Shan yu yi yi 善馭夷議
Shengwu ji 聖武記
shengxian 聖賢
shenhu 紳戶
shenjin 紳衿
shi 士
shidafu 士大夫
Shiguwei 詩古微
Shijing 詩經
shiren suoyan he zhi
    詩人所言何志
shunzhuang 順莊
shuyuan 書院
tankuan 攤款
Tao Shu 陶澍
ti 體
tianfu 田賦

Tian Wenjing 田文鏡
ting 亭
tonggou 統購
Tu Renshou 屠仁守
wangdao 王道
Wang Xiangyun 王湘雲
Wang Zhensheng 王振聲
Wei Yuan 魏源
Wenzheng 文徵
wu ba 五霸
wuchan 無產
wulun zhangu qingmian
    無論瞻顧情面
Wuxu bianfa 戊戌變法
xiangguan 鄉官
xiangting zhi zhi 鄉亭之制
xiangyue 鄉約
xiaoren 小人
xiashi 下士
xiedou 械斗
xiezhi 挾制
xing 興
Xinghua 興化
xinzheng 新政
xin zhongnong 新中農
xuehui 學會
xuepian 學篇

xuezhi yishuo 學治臆說
Yang Dapeng 楊大鵬
Yang Shixie 楊士爕
Yangwu yundong 洋務運動
Yanqing 延清
yifa 夷法
yilang 議郎
Ying zhao chenyan shu
    應詔陳言書
yiren tongdi 依人統地
yong 用
yuan 怨
Yutai 裕泰
Zhang Peilun 張佩綸
Zhao Erzhen 趙爾震
Zhao Liewen 趙烈文
zhenggou 征購
zhi pian 治篇
zhizhou 知州
zhongliu 中流
zhou 州
zhuan 專
zhupi zouzhe 硃批奏摺
ziqiang 自強
zizhi 自治
Zou Rong 鄒容

Index

agriculture, 26, 49, 95, 111; over-cultivation, 7, 32; in Soviet Union, 105; surplus production, 101, 102, 104, 106, 113, 133; during Great Leap Forward, 108–10. *See also* grain
American Congress, 63
ancestral halls, 84
apportioned funds (*tankuan*), 101
assemblies, 128
authoritarianism, 32, 66, 130, 132; evaluation of, 50; need for, 47, 51; protecting public interest, 70–71, 78

Bagehot, Walter, 17–18
Bao Shichen, 20
Beijing, 18–19, 69n, 117–19
Bo Yibo, 105n, 107
Board of Civil Appointment, 60
Book of Odes, The (*Shijing*), 34–42, 44, 118; "Brilliant Are the Flowers," 40; Confucius on, 38–39; constitutional significance of, 36; "Deer Call," 39–40, 95n; and empirical research school, 36; as mobilization tool, 39; modern/ancient text versions, 35–36, 37, 44, 45; other authors' use of, 36–37; as political communication, 39–40; significance of, 36–40, 44
Bosher, John Francis, 93n
Boxer Rebellion, 68, 113
Britain, 129, 130; Opium War, 3, 21, 32, 44, 52, 114n, 119; trade with China, 4
Buddhism, 7, 68
bureaucracy: able officials (*nengchen*), 44; centralization, 92–93; crafty officials (*qiaohuan*), 71; degree quotas, 15, 28; Donglin movement, 13–14;

false registration (*guiji*), 95
farmers, 6–7, 49; new middle
    peasants, 104; poverty of, 80–
    81; resentment of tax system,
    56–57. *See also* agriculture
Federalist, The ("Publius"), 73–78
fees. *See* surtaxes and fees
Fei Xiaotong, 111
Feng Guifen, 25, 55–79, 119, 130;
    admiration by Western schol-
    ars, 55; compared to Wei Yuan,
    55–56, 57, 61, 65; contemporary
    critics, 58–59, 66–70, 76, 78–79;
    early life and career, 55–57; *Es-
    says of Protest (Jiaobinlu kangyi)*,
    57–71; on grain transport tax,
    118; influence of Western ideas,
    58; nomination procedures for
    officials, 60–64, 68–69; pro-
    posals on middlemen, 64–67,
    72, 91, 126
fiscal policy and reforms: late im-
    perial, 95–96, 99; Republican
    era, 90–100; under PRC, 102–
    8, 133. *See also* economy
Fischer, Wolfram, 93n
Five Hegemons, 48–52
five-year plans, 107
floods, 4, 7, 32
foreign conquest, 124–25
foreign trade, 4, 6
France, 92–95

gentry managers, 72
Gong Shuduo, 59n
Gong Zizhen, 120
good works (*shanxing*), 77
government: boundaries of polity, 27–29, 48, 60; centralization, 45, 47, 130, 134–35; commercialization, 56, 80, 92, 95n,
97, 98, 99; frugality, 23, 24, 32;
modernization, 126; representa-
tional form, 123, 130–32; self-
government, 100–101, 126–32;
self-strengthening (*ziqiang*)
movement, 52, 55; Wei Yuan's
views on, 48–52; Western technologies, 52–53, 66, 100
grain: compulsory purchase
(*zhenggou*), 105–6; harmonious
purchase (*hedi*), 106n; procurement during Great Leap
Forward, 108–10; surplus, 101–
6, 113, 133; transport system,
20–21, 31, 51, 117–19; tribute
tax, 32, 46, 81, 91, 118; unified
purchase (*tonggou*), 105–6
Grain Transport Administration
(*caoyun*), 56–58, 65, 81, 117–19
Grand Canal, 117, 119
Grand Councilor. *See* Heshen
Grand Emperor. *See* Qianlong
Great Leap Forward, 108–11
Great Way (principles of wisdom), 40
Gu Yanwu, 36, 64–65, 77, 95n
Guangxu (emperor), 58
Guangzhou, 4, 21
Gunn, J. A. W., 76n
Guomindang, 102, 109, 111, 132
guwen (ancient text), 35n

Hamilton, Alexander, 74n
Han Chinese, 7, 9
Han Ying, 37